Also by Nancy Willard

NOVELS

Things Invisible to See

Sister Water

POETRY

In His Country

Skin of Grace

A New Herball

19 Masks for the Naked Poet

Carpenter of the Sun

Household Tales of Moon and Water

The Ballad of Biddy Early

Water Walker

*A Visit to William Blake's Inn: Poems for Innocent
and Experienced Travelers*

Among Angels (with Jane Yolen)

SHORT STORIES AND ESSAYS

Angel in the Parlor

Telling Time: Angels, Ancestors, and Stories

A Nancy Willard Reader

CRITICAL ESSAYS

Testimony of the Invisible Man

Swimming Lessons

Swimming Lessons

New and Selected Poems

NANCY WILLARD

ALFRED A. KNOPF   NEW YORK   1996

THIS IS A BORZOI BOOK PUBLISHED BY ALFRED A. KNOPF, INC.

Copyright © 1996 by Nancy Willard

All rights reserved under International and Pan-American
Copyright Conventions. Published in the United States by
Alfred A. Knopf, Inc., New York, and simultaneously in
Canada by Random House of Canada Limited, Toronto.
Distributed by Random House, Inc., New York.

http://www.randomhouse.com/

Owing to a limitation of space, all acknowledgments
and permissions for the reprinting of previously
published material may be found on page 209.

Library of Congress Cataloging-in-Publication Data
Willard, Nancy.
Swimming lessons : new and selected poems / by Nancy Willard—1st ed.
p.   cm.
ISBN 0-679-44639-7
I. Title
PS3573.I444S93   1996
811'.54—dc20   96-5760   CIP

Manufactured in the United States of America

First Edition

For Eric. Again.

I have a feeling that my boat
has struck, down there in the depths,
against a great thing.
                              And nothing
happens! Nothing . . . Silence . . . Waves . . .

Nothing happens! Or has everything happened,
and are we standing now, quietly in the new life?

—Juan Ramón Jiménez, "Oceans"

Contents

NEW POEMS

Swimming Lessons 3

Cold Water 5

At the Optometrist's 7

Grief and the Dentist 9

A Member of the Wedding 11

Memory Hat 12

The Patience of Bathtubs 14

Guesthouse, Union City, Michigan 15

Flea Market 16

Uninvited Houses 17

Fairy Tale 18

Swimming to China 19

The Exodus of Peaches 20

In Praise of the Puffball 22

The Alligator Wrestler 23

The Fruit Bat 25

Peacock Bride 26

The Wisdom of the Geese 27

The Wisdom of the Jellyfish 28

Sand Shark 29

Winston Farm 30

The Burning at Neilson's Farm 31

A Very Still Life 33

Still Life with Drive-in 34

The Bell Ringers of Kalamazoo 35

A Conversation Phrase Book for Angels 36

From a Postcard (found poem) 37

from IN HIS COUNTRY *(1966)*

The Flea Circus at Tivoli   41

Picture Puzzles   42

Marcel Marceau   45

Wedding Song   47

Bees Swarming   49

Saint Nicholas Is the Patron Saint of   50

"Ashes"   52

from *The Cycle of the Fountain (Oslo: Frogner Park)*   53

II. *"Kvinne og Enhjørning" (Woman and Unicorn)*

III. *"Gutt Kjemper Med Ørn" (Boy Fighting Eagle)*

V. *"Fontenen" (The Fountain)*

Camera Obscura   56

First Lesson   58

from SKIN OF GRACE *(1967)*

The Church   63

String Games   64

The Insects   66

Transcript, 1848   68

Guest   70

The Healers   71

Skin of Grace   72

from A NEW HERBALL *(1968)*

Moss   75

Arbor   77

Out of War   78

from 19 MASKS FOR THE NAKED POET *(1971)*

The Poet Takes a Photograph of His Heart 81

The Poet Invites the Moon for Supper 82

The Poet Writes Many Letters 83

The Poet Enters the Sleep of the Bees 84

The Poet Turns His Enemy into a Pair of Wings 85

The Poet Tracks Down the Moon 86

The Baker's Wife Tells His Horoscope with Pretzels 87

The Poet Stumbles upon the Astronomer's Orchards 88

The Poet's Wife Watches Him Enter the Eye of the Snow 89

from CARPENTER OF THE SUN *(1974)*

For You, Who Didn't Know 93

A Kind of Healing 95

Carpenter of the Sun 97

In Praise of ABC 98

A Humane Society 99

Walking Poem 101

Marriage Amulet 102

How to Stuff a Pepper 103

Roots 104

A Psalm for Running Water 106

In Praise of Unwashed Feet 107

The Animals Welcome Persephone 108

When There Were Trees 110

What the Grass Said 113

Clearing the Air 114

from HOUSEHOLD TALES OF MOON AND WATER *(1982)*

Questions My Son Asked Me, Answers I Never Gave Him 119

Night Light 121

Angels in Winter 123

Two Roman Goddesses 125

First goddess: Deverra

Second goddess: Juno Lucina

Lightness Remembered 128

How the Hen Sold Her Eggs to the Stingy Priest 130

Saint Pumpkin 131

The Sleep of the Painted Ladies 133

The Five Versions of the Icicle 134

Family Picnic with Wine and Water 135

Two Allegorical Figures 136

Country Scene 137

My Life on the Road with Bread and Water 138

In Which I Meet Bread and Catch Water

In Which Water Gathers the Full Moon

In Which Water Gives Me the Book of My Ancestors

In Which Water Turns Himself into a Feast

In Which I Leave Water and Find Road

Blessing for Letting Go

from THE BALLAD OF BIDDY EARLY *(1987)*

The Ballad of Biddy Early 147

How the Magic Bottle Gave Biddy Its Blessing 149

Charm of the Gold Road, the Silver Road, and the Hidden Road 151

How the Queen of the Gypsies Met Trouble-and-Pain 152

How Biddy Called Back Friday, Her Lost Pig   154
Biddy Early Makes a Long Story Short   155
Song from the Far Side of Sleep   156

from WATER WALKER *(1989)*
A Wreath to the Fish   159
The Feast of St. Tortoise   160
Psalm to the Newt   161
Airport Lobsters   162
Life at Sea: The Naming of Fish   163
Poem Made of Water   165
A Hardware Store as Proof of the Existence of God   167
Missionaries Among the Heathen   168
Memorial Day in Union City, Michigan   170
Science Fiction   171
Coming to the Depot   172
The Teachings of the Jade   174
A Psalm for Vineyards   175
Onionlight   176
The Potato Picker   177
The Weeder   178
God Enters the Swept Field   179
Small Medicinal Poem   180
For Karen   182
Little Elegy with Books and Beasts   183

Poems from the Sports Page   185
"Buffalo Climbs out of Cellar"
"Saints Lose Back"
"Field Collapses Behind Patullo"

"Tigers Shake Up Pitchers Again"
"Wayward Lass Wins Mother Goose"
"Stars Nip Wings"
"Divine Child Rolls On"

from A NANCY WILLARD READER *(1991)*

One for the Road 195

from AMONG ANGELS *(1995)*

The Winged Ones 199
Photographing the Angels 200
Angels Among the Servants 202
Jacob Boehme and the Angel 204
Visitation in a Pewter Dish 206

New Poems

Swimming Lessons

A mile across the lake, the horizon bare
or nearly so: a broken sentence of birches.
No sand. No voices calling me back.
Waves small and polite as your newly washed hair
push the slime-furred pebbles like pawns,
an inch here. Or there.

You threaded five balsa blocks on a strap
and buckled them to my waist, a crazy life
vest for your lazy little daughter.
Under me, green deepened to black.
You said, "Swim out to the deep water."
I was seven years old. I paddled forth

and the water held me. Sunday you took away
one block, the front one. I stared down
at my legs, so small, so nervous and pale,
not fit for a place without roads.
Nothing in these depths had legs or need of them
except the toeless foot of the snail.

Tuesday you took away two more blocks.
Now I could somersault and stretch.
I could scratch myself against trees like a cat.
I even made peace with the weeds that fetch
swimmers in the noose of their stems
while the cold lake puckers and preens.

Friday the fourth block broke free. "Let it go,"
you said. When I asked you to take
out the block that kept jabbing my heart,

I felt strong. This was the sixth day.
For a week I wore the only part
of the vest that bothered to stay:

a canvas strap with nothing to carry.
The day I swam away from our safe shore,
you followed from far off, your stealthy oar
raised, ready to ferry me home
if the lake tried to keep me.
Now I watch the tides of your body

pull back from the hospital sheets.
"Let it go," you said. "Let it go."
My heart is not afraid of deep water.
It is wearing its life vest,
that invisible garment of love
and trust, and it tells you this story.

Cold Water

When I found the stream in the woods
I plunged my face in and drank
like the slow machinery of cows
who camp on the shadows of trees,
drowsy as soldiers on a day
without danger, without death.
My tongue scrolled up water
as if I could pack it and save
contentment for when I'd need it.
The fans of the aspens fluttered.
I put my mouth on the sun
where the water sharpens its claws
on the slippery rocks and tasted
the hunger of herons who study
the rippling signature of water
and crack the code of the trout.
I rolled the stream in my mouth.
Somewhere clouds crossed the peaked
and rumpled sea and carried
the rain in their cheeks like light:
water so used, so homely
I savored my own birth.
I cupped my hands and sipped
from a cold pocket and tasted
a cracked skull in a lake
and bodies, skewered and split,
that rolled in the current's arms
in Rwanda, in Uganda,
in Lake Victoria, Lake Victoria.
When water hyacinths loosed them,

stinking, they eddied ashore.
And now their death washes
through every atom of me.
Beloved, if you kiss me,
everything we love
will swim in it.

At the Optometrist's

This is a fearful place.
From the lit shelves stare
a hundred eyeglasses—
the voyeurs fled but left
their startled glances.

Vigilantes of the Second Coming,
they have their reward.
In the twinkling of an eye
we shall all be changed.
And everything twinkles here,
the dynasties of gold frames

in the tricky mirrors,
the tinted lenses on velvet
plates, like the scales
said to fall from our eyes
in moments of truth.

No bait catches the fish
who swims in invisible waters.
The scales he sheds
are powerful slices of light.
"Pick your frames," says the doctor,
who loves to paint

and for their burnished gold
leaf frames buys old
landscapes lost to sight

under cataracts of varnish.
The frames he hands me weigh

less than the sparrow
whose engine of small bones
I buried last April
under the bare maples,
all of us squinting
into the new light.

Grief and the Dentist

Am I the main course?
How his cutlery shines,
his pick a question mark,
his mirror a moon caught

on a silver baton.
In his wickless lamp
a flame broods, ghostly
over a silver mouth.

Has it crouched there long?
Shall I be done to a turn?
The pain in my tooth:
I thought it was larger

than this wriggling filament
from an old light bulb
drawn in silence
from its damp chamber,

which the dentist dangles
for my approval. "This
is the root of the problem."
He points to the nerve—

a serpent plucked
from a porcelain box

neither safe nor beautiful,
its crown a bleached cabbage,

its two-legged root
clumsy as pliers,
the fire out,
the tomb empty.

A Member of the Wedding

If I could remove the head of the man in front of me,
I'd see the bride instead of her proud father,
her glad father instead of the nervous groom,
the nimble groom instead of the deaf priest,
the slow priest instead of the sprinkled water,
the blessed water instead of the wrinkled sea,
the wide sea instead of the crowded sky,
the mackerel sky instead of the wheeling sun,
the dealing sun instead of the drumming moon,
the bald moon, bride of heaven,
beautiful in her emptiness,
beautiful with nothing to hide,
beautiful as the head of the man in front of me,
beautiful as the bride.

Memory Hat

"Do not pack, flatten or fold the Memory Hat as it will retain the altered shape."
—Care Instructions for
a Panama Hat

Headhunter, traveler,
Sombrero de paja toquilla,
hat of the straw headdress,
your brim so broad I am
a shady character, gossiping
to the stunned ears of orchids
and the folded ears of cats,
to lilies with no discretion
and whelks that remember nothing
but what your brim bargained:
Your secret is safe with me.
Keep it under your hat.

Priest of palmettos
and patron saint of haberdashers,
born like a galaxy from a navel
in the moist air of the mountains,
crowned without thorns,
brimming with beauty at last,
accept my head, Saint Panama Hat.
Holy martyr, washed, bleached,
steamed, stretched on the rack,
every fiber obedient, trained.
I vow to preserve you,
all the days of your life,

never to leave you on the window shelf of a car,
never to abandon you to an arid embrace,

never to flatten or fold you.
And when we are tired of each other,
I will boil water in a pot and steam you,

I will sing the last words of lobsters
as they sink into suffering,
their carapace crimson, their flesh a cream,
and you will shrink or stretch,
and I will place you in the sun,
in the curved arm of time
brimmed in eternity, shading the hill

of my head that considers the sky
as it throws down light, bundles of it,
on the tender riddle of hats.

The Patience of Bathtubs

I admire the patience of bathtubs,
their humility, their grace under pressure.
I have seen bathtubs like melancholy tureens
into which the moon ladles her light broth.
The saint who sailed from Ireland in a bathtub
found the Blessed Isles, and no wonder.

A strange tub once adopted me, carried me
for hours in its magnificent belly,
gurgled for joy when I pulled the plug,
and filled it—oh, Zen disciple—with emptiness.
How it crouched on four chilly legs,
a snowshoe hare in hiding from hunters

or a white cat willing the wren's breath
to make a small stir in the hedge,
like that Roman fountain in the Hyde,
marble-mouthed, leaf-lipped, muttering water,
filling the chaste basin with off-color stories
leaving their rusty breath on the streaked stone.

Guesthouse, Union City, Michigan

What strange soap! Like a chunk
of amber that windows a scarab's sleep,
it smells like nothing
but the hand that holds it,

though it lathers me in light
and loves nothing in this house,
not the best china in the small theatre
of the cabinet, or the draperies

dead from years of keeping
the darkness in, or the jars
of silence lacquered with fragrance,
or the ghost of my grandmother

watching over this house
in which things are done right
and paying guests sleep dreamless
under their own stars.

Flea Market

I

Records freed from their jackets
scratched past hearing, a table
of oil lamps, doors with the screens ripped out
marshaled and stacked, opening to each other,
clothes scattered in piles across the field,
as if when the flood pulled back,
the living returned to nothing
but what God couldn't carry or didn't love.

2

After my mother taught me to swim
I dove deep for what people lost:
a silver spoon, a rusty rod that harrowed
and hooked weeds, eyeglasses gleaming in muck
till I freed them, not for money
but because they had come so far, like dinner plates
gliding through portholes that leave behind
the indestructible ship with its cargo of corpses.

3

A vacuum cleaner upright among the thistles
imagines its greatest work is still to come.
I remember my mother urging the Hoover forward,
up and down, as if she were ploughing the rug,
erasing dust, hair, nail parings, spittle.

How much my mother left me. And how little.

Uninvited Houses

for Joan Gold

The houses kept coming
into her paintings, though she tried
to stop them, though she asked
the two barns, one male, one female,
who stepped from her mauve sky,
"Who are you? What country sent you?"
So many begged her to make them

visible; a silo packed
with the sawdust of twilight,
an ark sent to deliver the morning,
after her father died
clutching his Star of David
and his crucifix.
He is the guardhouse with a red roof

and a gate to the city of steeples.
He is the sky peeling itself to glory.
While her friend was dying, she painted
many safe places for her to be glad in,
tents stitched from the silks of riders
who raced hard and won. The last house
was a shadow of itself, the ghost

razed to sight on the wall after
a demolition. When it opened
a window, someone left
a blue plate on the sill.
What shines so? The bright
hem of the door answers:
open all night.

Fairy Tale

When you light a fire, I draw near like a cat,
crouching on warm bricks till the embers die.

I do not know the way of making fires,
only of prodding the logs and pushing the ashes together.

Sometimes the great logs twitter before they fall,
and I poke the ashes, looking for trapped birds

who fell in the fire but went on singing.
And if a white bear steps from the morning's throat

may I be still enough to hear him,
may I be warm enough to invite him in.

Swimming to China

To touch hair that gleams
like piano keys (black ones);
to live among porcelain gods
in whose hands peaches are scepters;
to eat rice with ginger
like slices of damp amber, using
two happy batons; to desire squid,
pickled leeks, shark soup;
to eat a bird's nest and taste patience;
to find the moon in my beancurd cake,

a boiled yolk like a ball in a well;
to hide soapstone monkeys
in a lacquered chest,
to open its jade doors
and find more than I looked for,
water chestnuts at prayer,
a teacup scarfed in dragons,
fans cracking their knuckles,
and a packet of paper fish
on which someone has written,

We are flowers.
Put us back in the water.

The Exodus of Peaches

The new peach trees are bandaged
like the legs of stallions.

You can read the bark
over the tape's white lip

where its russet Braille
is peeling. The peaches hang

in their green cupolas,
cheeks stained with twilight,

the wind stencilled on velvet
livery. What a traffic

of coaches without wheels,
of bells without tongues!

Far off the barn doors
open, close,

open, close.
An argument,

both sides swinging.
The blue tractor zippers the field

and disappears behind slatted boxes
like weathered shingles, stained

with peach juice.
I stood under peaches

clumped close as barnacles,
loyal as bees,

and picked one
from the only life it knew.

In Praise of the Puffball

The puffball appears on the hill
like the brain of an angel,
full of itself yet modest,
where it sprang like a pearl
from the dark fingers of space
and the ring where light years ago
it clustered unnoticed,
a gleam in the brim of Saturn,

a moon as homely as soap,
scrubbed by solar winds
and the long shadows of stars
and the smoke of dead cities
and the muscles of the tide
and the whorled oil of our thumbs,
and the earth, pleased to make room
for this pale guest, darkening.

The Alligator Wrestler

The alligator waits in her aluminum case,
shaped to hold the odd length of her
like a troubled trombone. When her keeper
cracks open the lid, anger leaches out
in hopeless coils, like the roots
of mangroves buckled and snarled.

Her mouth's tied. Two men heave her
pale body, bear it to the clearing,
and cut her free. Stunned by the dry grass
and the trampled light, she hisses—
is she dying of a punctured heart?
Her jaws unfold, pink and gleaming

and strange as a porcelain ironing board.
She fills herself with sunlight
till the keeper makes a move
on her. Then she slams herself shut.
Grabbing her snout, he sinks his fingers
under her creamy jaw and straddles her.

Her throat is mild and naked as a glove.
Flipped on her back, she's out cold.
Now we admire her head, slim
as a beak, her moon-white belly tiled

like the floor of the shower
in some dingy Y. "In this position,"

says her keeper, "the blood is leaving
her brain. In this position, she could die."
He nuzzles her cobbled ear, calling
in the sweet tongue by which alligators
choose each other. Her tail twitches.
She's back. The show is over.

The Fruit Bat

Because the air has darkened
like bruised fruit, you creep
down the bare branch

where you slept all light long,
gathered into yourself like a fig.
Little mandarin woman fleeing

under the stars on bound feet,
when your wings spring open
even you look surprised.

What are the raven's slick feathers
beside these pewter sails
raised in the foundry of your flesh,

burnished by light poured
from a wasted moon and a dipper
brimming with darkness?

Peacock Bride

The peacock bride comes in drag
to the gate, dragging his blue train
through the blond grass, flattening it.

Distracted, he snaps off a leaf,
a stem. His foolish crown shakes
its fistful of antennae but stays put.

I think he is mad.
It is hot, the field is empty,
and here comes the bride

in a riverbrown shawl. Oh, he wears
too much make-up; a creamy
center-of-the-road stripe circles

his eyes. They scan me,
and seeing I mean no harm
he stretches the blue mast of his neck

and sails away into the sunny field.

The Wisdom of the Geese

The geese are displeased.
They want to invent the snow.

Each has swallowed
a whole pitcher of light.

Stuffed with brightness,
they can hardly move.

As they waddle through tall grass
they drop feathers, quaint clues,

like the arch humor of ferns.
Something wakes the pond, wrinkling it.

It's bad luck to look back.
They step off into dark water.

The Wisdom of the Jellyfish

The moon sheds its skin, knitting
halos and casting them off.
On the beach, how they shine

and pulse and glisten
like the fontanels of the newborn.
What is it to be a lens

focused on the feathery star
of your own life,
fireworks trapped

in a bruised sky?
As you shrink to a coin
minted in lace, you dry

to a chalky spill. The sea
smooths things over.
Look inward, says the jellyfish.

I am all eyes, God-sighted.
I peacock the land. When I died,
I showed you the whole galaxy.

Sand Shark

Sealed in your pewter coat,
your belly white
as a starched cuff,
you died in the tracks

drawn by your dorsal fin
as you heaved at low tide
toward pages of water
turning and turning.

I could read by the light
that pours from your sockets.
Picked clean, they open
on bony chambers crammed

with roses that darken
behind your nostrils,
finely drawn on the rounded
cone of your nose, like

needle holes left
by stitches so small
even your breath
couldn't find them.

Winston Farm

The barn falls slowly but not under fire.
It gives itself up to a cargo
of toppled turrets, ladders supporting

the ruffled nests of wasps and grape
tendrils tangled as barbed wire.

A roof thatched with feathers would keep
out the rain better than this one.
With no one to save them, the walnuts lie

where they fell, bigger than musket balls
and pungent. The stable's still

standing. The bridles and bits dangle
in the stalls, over which someone
has printed the names *Beauty, Lance,*

like the dead at Gettysburg whose names
penciled on old planks saved

what was left of them under those shields
when the living went out to harvest
their dead on a morning like this one,

moving quietly over the cropped fields.

The Burning at Neilson's Farm

Saratoga Battlefield

Something lives here, has burrowed
into the burned hill, pushing the blond
earth out like light torn
from a black hole or the sour grave

of a boot. Quickgrass and rye
rot where they fell—hair heaped
on the barber's floor, a scatter
of pewtery ash, of eyelashes feeling

for lost lights. On the road
through the battlefield the crew is resting.
The ranger goes on eating his lunch,
leaning against his truck. Its painted

camouflage looks new. He orders
the burning of fields between two cannons
clean as fountains, patina
polished to jade. In blackened fields

the newer monuments mark time,
or the end of it. Gates to the hereafter:
Here the battle raged back and forth,
here Major Acland was wounded—

Here lie events, not men. Too many fell
to keep track of. In the ravine

the stream's off and running. Sprung
birches fall into each other's arms,

their torn jackets coiled, keeping the shape
of broken logs rotting away inside.
Beech saplings flutter their pale flags,
burrs give out sharp reports. The red coats

on the new dogwood stems glisten.
The pampas grass, its dry plumes
broken or bent, surrenders.
There's thunder. Water puts out fire.

In the ravine, beyond the milkweed field,
lichens inch out their lives in milky rings.
I watch the grey pods set their feathers free,
as if the broken sky laid down its wings.

A Very Still Life

Lake Michigan

Over that dune lies the water, its engines
turned off for the winter, its winks and
rumples stilled.

The clouds come home dreaming of it, making
signs to the trees: a great thing lives
out there.

It wears the world's dirty linen. Mudded,
forgotten, it stands up like a camel.
The snow

goes on wooling it. The tips
of broken bottles pock it—
chimneys

of lost bunkers. You can't guess
how quiet it is. A woman from town
walks

its ridges. Even the slat-fence
that keeps the beach open disobeys,
lies down.

Still Life with Drive-in

The drive-in has lost face,
though its speakers stand
at attention in the vacant field

to which no one comes
even to harvest silence.
An abandoned tomb:

the screen throws its shade
on the crowd, foxtail and vetch.
But even the sunflowers

are looking the other way.
Nevertheless, it was here she first
listened to her heart,

faithful chaperone
keeping watch over her as a boy's hands
raced across ripe fields of her flesh,

under those huge lovers in heaven
whose hot breath, piped into the car,
filled it, though she could still hear

her heart ticking off each word:
    Down here, the stars fade.
    Down here you too will ride off
    into the shadows.

The Bell Ringers of Kalamazoo

In the round tower the ropes hang at rest.

Seven nooses drop from the ceiling in this cell
a monk would hold dear because the roots
of a vine seem to dwell here, whose blossoms

are seven bells hidden in the high dark
to which I shall be hauled if I hold
to one rope while the bell, ringing, turns over,

all five tons of it; whose vocal cord
I hold in my hand, ready for a true peal,
ready to pass through the gates of "Plain Bob,"

"Kent," "St. Dunstan," hunting the lines down,
seven bells braiding and unbraiding the tunes.
If I could ring the book of Kells I would have

ringers bowing and stretching, and we would climb
the ladder through the ceiling into the cramped
nest of the bells we are forbidden to touch,

so carefully are they balanced on their wheels,
brooding, blind in their plumage of graven
mottos: *Make a joyful noise.*

I will dwell in the house
of righteousness forever.
Lux est.

A Conversation Phrase Book
for Angels

Telling the Time

The moon has discovered the mud in the old pasture.
Moon-tracks cover the little wallow with crescents.
What shall we do if the brown horse leaves us?
Her shadow is five hours new and cannot stand alone.
Her glad tail marks time for the whole vineyard.
Would you know this for a vineyard if I did not tell you?
Every evening the horse turns into a table
and bears the bread of astonishment over the hill.

Foretelling the Weather

Something has seeded the farmer's field with stones.
A stone wall grows fast, a stone grows faster.
His wine forgets it was born in his eldest field.
While his vines are telling their beads, the cold kills them.
Note how the mare's tail sweeps and swabs.
The milkweed empties its purse crammed with moon-skins.
Her pasture gathers the shiny bones of the stars.
If the sky calls, she will lie down in it.

From a Postcard (found poem)

Jan 2, 1918
Greenfield, New York

Auntie just read your letter.
Help yourself to the apples.
She wants you to take the potatoes
if you need them
if they are any good.

There is a basket of eggs
in the cellarway on the shelf.
Take those too.

And help yourself to all the flour
you want. There is a sack of sugar
you might as well have.
It is in the kitchen cabinet.

Isn't it cold?
We spend most of the time shoveling
coal in the furnace.
Auntie feels good and is

contented.

from

In His Country

(1966)

The Flea Circus at Tivoli

Let a saint cry your praises, O delicate
desert companion, the flea.
So tiny a mover ruffles his faith
and sends him, scratching and singing,
praising the smallest acrobats of God.

The lady with alligator hips and
hummingbirds in her hair, tramples invisible trumpets.
The lights in her eyes dim.
Now from an ivory box her tweezers pluck
three golden chariots and a cycle, spoked
like a spider, drumming the swath of green.

"Behold," cries the lady with delphinium voice,
"Olaf and Alfred and Madame Wu, three fleas
of ancient lineage, fed at my own breast
will race to this miniature castle of pearls."
In the twilight of her eyes, the gold
wagons advance, cautious as caterpillars.

But for the drivers, who can describe
them, save that each carriage moves?
That a golden bicycle whirls forever
toward heaven, moved by invisible hands?
"For those who doubt, here is a glass
which reveals the cause of the tiniest motions."

But clearer than any glass, we believe,
we admire their wizard beaks and their tiny legs
pumping the wheels hard, their gardens and parliaments,
pleasing as postage stamps, commemorative,
and we go out praising.

Picture Puzzles

It's because we're broken
that we love
   puzzles; pictures
cut all askew, fifteen hundred
   pieces, salvage
of divine catastrophe.
   For two dollars my mother
buys, in good faith,
   Fra Angelico's Nativity,
incredibly cracked,
   sung
like God's defense
   on a skeptic's tongue.

   Bishops consecrating
earth newly broken
   for things not known or seen,
we scatter the pieces
   upon a table and begin
the impossible assemblage.
   Peacocks, kings, horses
sleep in the rubble, peasants,
   angels, and gillyflowers
cocked for resurrection.
   Pieces like grey stones,
piece like a bloody star,
   pieces like bones.

   First the borders of green appear.
Through a thaw
   in the senseless floes

breaks
the crimson robe
of an angel.
Excavating
a lost language,
we dredge
for the verb that binds
image to image in one word,
clear
sheaf in the maker's mind.

Always the possibility
that someone may disturb us—the dog
kick the table,
the baby
trample the pieces together,
stones thrown
in the ponds of our peace.
Patient, as if
we brought from our bombed cellars
the glass anatomy of the saints
at Chartres, at Notre Dame
we heal with light their voices
so often maimed.

The saint, the king flowers
not from our knowing but our being born.
We know
we make the picture to find again

the simple paradise
　　of Fra Angelico,
hymning in broken chords
　　how without this bloody star
the angel could not stand,
　　how the shapes of our healing lie
　　dumb in our hand.

Marcel Marceau

From the mime I learn to believe
in the certain weight
of what is certainly not there.
I gasp
that a teacup should fall
crashless as cotton.
And because I know the trial
of a cage, the clasp
of a shawl,
the quaint forgotten
peace that settles a park,
I know these in the dark
spaces where his arms smile,
as God, among philosophers,
thrives on denial.

When his hands flutter into birds
by imitation, that is, a construct
of faith and much seeing
of many wings
I know my grandmother tells
the truth, though the words falter
when we sit chilled in the lean
rough pews and the priest sings,
shaking sweet savor and bells.
Now the angels are crowding the altar.
And I, who have never seen
the gold feathers of prayer

know the shape of my own fear
burning like candles that suffer
my eyes with long lights after the hiss
of the deacon's snuffer.

I know that unbelievers
are most passionate, most aware
that there are false miracles
and true:
the invisible servants that steal
the letter you meant to send
press for belief
by concealment of cause and clue.
The absence, more real,
of a shell in the hand
shows in relief
the footprint of sense and motion.
So out of long devotion
to love we refine
ourselves, absent even to ourselves,
feeling ourselves changed, the beast
sings like an angel, water into wine,
by long fasting, finds the wedding feast.

Wedding Song

Orpheus calling. The grass parts, the seas
  lie down for Orpheus, the one
    calling, without harp or hymn,
      with his favored flesh, running
        white as a summer's day,

warmer than grass and stone
  where the sun lay.
    Everyone running, running before
      Orpheus, who loses again
        and again, himself, calling.

The grove beats with voices, sees
  a wedding walking, trees
    harping and crying, Eurydice
      runs in a white dress, her train
        catching the burrs and the leaves falling.

We, strangers on a bridge, look down.
  The moss-wedded water shows
    a wedding walking through water cress
      and wild flags, turning, flows
        into the muddy bed.

Procession in weedy dress
  spins us around too late. For us
    the air burns with their having
      been, like a swing rocking
        where the child has fled.

The serpent that gnaws
   at love lies sunning
      in the song. Orpheus calling.
         Through the woods they pass,
            hand in hand, running,

the word calling, the grass
   parts and the sea lies down
      before the hymn, himself, before
         this man who loves, who was
            before sea, grass, and all falling.

Bees Swarming

Just at noon in the summer I hear them.
Behind the house the hives stare
like tombstones in the tall grass.
But a small hum rises in the air,

high hymn of women in a wooden church.
Their gathering swells in the long heat.
Now they hang on the air like a pouch of gold,
singers and sextons of the plum and wheat.

My grandfather covers himself with black,
eclipses himself in a net to his knees,
costume that cries, I am invisible,
the hooded hunter of the innocent bees.

The net in his hand leaps and the glaze of noise
contracts to a frantic ball.
Now I hear nothing but cries and lament,
bodies and wings as they fall.

"So it must be," says my grandfather,
doffing his net and his hood—he is not
a cruel man. "So it must be.
If they are to make the gold, they must be caught

and made to live in the dark hive.
That's where the apple and plum
change to mineral sweetness
and divisible sun."

Saint Nicholas Is the Patron Saint of

children and scholars, by virtue
of a subtle likeness
acknowledged by neither.

I have seen scholars fall
in love with the print
and forget the poem
as children, unwrapping a costly doll
are most pleased
with the small tag on its gown:
"cleans with ease."

The worth of a guinea springs
from no solvent powers.
Its cameo world rejoices,
is therefore saved,
ranking with shells and with pressed flowers,
amphoras, apes'
skulls, words, and wings
not to fly with but to delight
the eye as things,
caps and categories loved
for their smooth shapes
and voices
calling nouns home for the night.

Patron saint
of order where none appears,
of a forest which neither sees:

children bend homes in the trees
and scholars, gathering mushrooms, fear
the fat man who abuses
their harpsichord hearts in a stew,
the lean man who cries
their colors as speechless white.

Their order belongs to eyes
that the earth chooses
to edit a work much vexed:
            de verietate rerum,
an occult, particular text.

"Ashes"

Edvard Munch

Like a borough of owls, the forest calls
and he calls it wise. He knows
how at its heart the light falls
like judgment on what it shows.

Turning, he sees through the cage of trees
ships like decoys threading an open bay.
  "You will leave me again and again. You must stay.
  You must give yourself to no one but me.
  Take this ring. Never forget the day,
  nor me, your dear beast, waiting in this wood.
  If you fail our meeting, I shall go away."

Already he looks at summer and longs for spring.
  "Say that I failed her who was fierce and good
  to me; that I came late but that I wore the ring,
  even to ashes, to the other side.
  Say that her claws shaped
  my heart till molder and metal cried.
  Say that the forest took her, that I escaped."

from *The Cycle of the Fountain (Oslo: Frogner Park)*

Gustav Vigeland's sculptures

II
"Kvinne og Enhjørning" (Woman and Unicorn)

In the peaceable kingdom, discord is not
absent but not understood. The lambs chase
after the leopard, the wolves trot
at the kids' heels. The air is thin
and musical; natures forgive. The hand
of a suckling child on the serpent's den
cries danger only to men
whose knowledge grew in a different place.

You, lying awake at night, recall
how broken tombs apologized that kings
bound for Elysium, moved nowhere at all
but lay withered in sleep with costly things.
If it is not here, it is nowhere, then.
But the woman beside you asleep
is riding the black bear into holiness
with her friends, the unicorn and the sheep,
as if the old herdsman will never call
home every creature from them and from you.

Only the gods rise with the dew.
You must go through water to meet them,
or at least be born in the image you grieve

to see, seeing over your shoulder how all
things follow the herdsman, taking their leave,
not knowing they leave to join the dead.
The woman is waking now but cannot tell
you one word that the unicorn said.

III
"Gutt Kjemper Med Ørn" (Boy Fighting Eagle)

As a young man he fights a beast with wings.
They meet on the hill of his heart. Its paws
grasp him hard, yet not to win
so much as hold him still.
Whether it loves or fears him,
he cannot tell.

In sleep it seems to bear him away,
singing to him of its ancient home.
Have you forgotten how we two played then?
The bear ran at your call and the deer and the sun.
Even the wolf was tame.

As the wings hollow for flight, a hawk's cry
calls him back, and the young man chooses
and cuts down the life of his strangest prey.
Now it is the wolf he fights, and he loses.

V

"Fontenen" (The Fountain)

"*Sursum corda;* I will rejoice evermore."
  The bird flies through the trees, the herdsman sleeps,
  and the children falling blind us like snow.
  The tomb in the hill smiles, its green door

  calling the piper to come, and keeps
  them still, though we have lost the way.
  For beyond this tree, who can stay?
  Who are those watching us that race

  our distance with a sunbeam's tread?
  The bird falls but the trees spread
  their boughs for new ones, and the old kings
  who shot them thought the game worthwhile.

Their death masks smile:
    We do not know the herdsman's face.
    It is your own heart, in all falling things,
    that calls you singing to the banquet door.
    Sursum corda; you shall rejoice evermore.

Camera Obscura

Photographer,
midwife
to the beautiful and the stillborn,
when you have covered the windows
against all natural light
you are ready to begin
these unnatural resurrections.

The tray of acid hisses.
The red safe light shows
the hands of an assassin
and their fastidious crime
against memory, against natural law.

You dust the negative:
the inner garment of time
which reverses our knowledge.
It bleaches
his dark hair white,
it bruises
his white shirt black,
and shows me
nothing that I remember.

You dip the blank page
into the fluid
from which these things are born
and we wait
like sitters at a seance,
calling the image of one we loved.

And now through the water,
through blizzards of nonbeing,

through the painful changes
like green fruit ripening,
like a summer
which did not ask to return,
surprised in its shroud,
its sealed forgetfulness torn,
he rises,
obeying the summons,
darkening, gaining strength and depth
like an excellent wine:

A boy on the Brooklyn Bridge, smiling
because the Empire State and the Chase Manhattan
and the Stock Exchange and St. Patrick's
stand on the shore
like a congregation of bishops
sent to welcome the traveler
from across the water.

A boy looking up at us
from the bed of a drowned man,
his gaze deflected
by invisible currents,
transfixed in the midst
of his route to a totaler darkness.
You intercede
for this innocent condemned.
You have saved
a messenger
with the face of a dead friend.

First Lesson

*So I studied the egg, and everything I
learned came from that study.*
—Constantin Brancusi

Holding this egg,
    detail
of Quaker plainness,
    familiar
as thee and thou,
    I hold the color and shape
of peace,
    whether blown and dyed,
balloon promising flight
    that a finger crunkles,
or boxed, the lid raised to show
    a jury noncommittal
as the bald heads of
    a dozen uncles.

The shape of peace
    is the certainty
of the simple thing:
    as when a man draws
one line, known
    from the first
and it opens what we forgot.
    Unicorn understood
from the magnificent horn,
    so I know flight
without wings
    when a candle
against the shell shows
    only a milky light.

"Learn from the egg
      and the bird's wing,"
observed Brancusi, flapping
      about his room in red
sandals, his garden of
      sculpted birds spinning
on pedestals like patient
      and sleepy bears.
Tortoise of turquoise,
      birds waking in brass
and silver, harp
      that leaps from the bowels
of Orpheus
      says,

I am a harp raised
      to the first joy of my master's mind,
falling into myself like water
      and sleeping child.
Make birds, wings, planets,
      minerals, faces; nothing you gather
will sing so clearly
      how we are alive, nothing praise
the flight of a bird
      so well as this
round possibility,
      silence unshattered, temple soon
to be raised, the
      ancient word.

from

Skin of Grace

(1967)

The Church

If the walls are whitewashed clean, I hope
that under the show of purity I can find
a mural of monkeys pressing wine,
that below the candles on the choir stall

someone has carved a dancing bear or a girl
riding a wild boar.
The hands that made the dragon under the
saint's feet must know the dragon is

beautiful. And therefore, on the altar,
the Bible will rest on the back of a griffin
to remind you the beast is present
in every birth.

You shall not exclude them from the communion
of saints and men. If the roof is plain
put a cock on the steeple; you shall not
exclude them from your marriages.

String Games

More like a harp than a hammock,
the cat's cradle holds no cat but sags

its warp on a child's
fingers. "It wouldn't warm a mouse,"
says the old woman, her needles
chattering over the slow growth

of sweaters and socks, useful
as lexicons and oatmeal.

It's not to warm anything that
you gather and fold the string
but to hold the Protean act
together, shaking it

inside out: tennis court for
a party of moths, hopscotch,

the stick figures that your mind
makes between stars, meeting
each night Orion's belt and
the Water Bearer whose elbow turns

a million miles from her boneless
wrist. None of my lexicons knows

how the string goes
to this place, rapid as argument,
acrobatic as a conversation
of mutes. It leaves nothing behind,

arrives with nothing, stands
nowhere but ravels its simple cradles

and familiar space like proverbs
struck on your hands.

The Insects

They pass like a warning of snow,
    the dragonfly, mother of millions,
the scarab, the shepherd spider,
    the bee. Our boundaries break
on their jeweled eyes,
    blind as reflectors.
The black beetle
    under the microscope wears the
blue of Chartres. The armored
    mantis, a tank in clover,
folds its wings like a flawless
    inlay of wood, over and over.

"There is something about insects
    that does not belong to the habits
of our globe," said Maeterlinck,
    touching the slick
upholstery of the spider,
    the watchspring and cunning
tongue of the butterfly, blown out
    like a paper bugle. Their humming
warns us of sickness, their silence
    of honey and frost. Asleep
in clapboards and rafters,
    their bodies keep

the cost of our apples and wool.
    A hand smashes their wings,

tearing the veined
    landscape of winter trees.
In the slow oozing of our days
    who can avoid remembering
their silken tents on the air,
    the spiders wearing their eggs
like pearls, born on muscles
    of silk, the pulse of a rose, baiting
the moth that lives for three hours,
    lives only for mating?

Under a burning glass, the creature
    we understood disappears. The dragonfly
is a hawk, the roach
    cocks his enormous legs at your acre,
eyes like turrets piercing
    eons of chitin and shale. Drummers
under the earth, the cicadas
    have waited for seventeen summers
to break their shell,
    shape of your oldest fear
of a first world
    of monsters. We are not here.

Transcript, 1848

I think none of us knew her; yet everyone
knew the girl from Amherst, young for her class,
dark hair severely parted, attendance
somewhat irregular, for which
she came, reserved and sullen, to my office.
When she lifted her head, you saw the eyes
of a surgeon parsing your spirit. Once a law

student arrived, asking for Miss Dickinson, and she,
sprigged and awkward, served tea; I was
astonished, thinking she had no one. Curling
her lip slightly, she read the class
her essay on Pope, brilliant and strange,
into which she dissolved like a shower of sparks.
In chapel, she knelt with her hands clenched

rather than folded. The gentleman caller
did not come again; "I had a friend who taught
me Immortality, but venturing too near,
himself, he never returned."
During the retreat for penitents,
I looked out and saw her,
cutting across the forbidden grass,

making, as usual, her own path.
Prayers in her mouth crumbled to clay;
Christ and the Trinity might have been
the jam pot, the butter on
the table, a good book. During a reprimand

she stared angrily, pitifully out at flowers.
Standing at my door, waiting to see me,

not knocking, but listening for the sound of
my breath on the other side, she seemed
—how shall I call her?—ghostly, waking to
terror in the grey chill of the class
and the patient responses of pupils dozing,
while she, flayed by the new space, felt the air
nailing her down, then the final closing.

Guest

When you bring in the hyacinth,
the room

fills up with fragrance. At night
if you cross

the place where it prints
its shadow,

it prickles your skin: pasture
and white

breathing of stones.
Come in.

The Healers

for Helen Siegl

Under your foot at dusk, smell
the compassionate herbs. Their being

is being broken for our need.
Periwinkle, joy of the ground

"maketh a meek stomach and a good heart."
Caraway in comfits, fennel and seed

of vervain, the simples of grace,
heal us of witchcraft and wagging teeth.

Comforters of the aged and blind,
you make the sinner chaste.

Carried like a staff, you open the dark.
Watchman, what of the night? And you

the servant whose waiting we hardly see:
I am here. Take me.

Skin of Grace

It will have the color of clod,
    the smell of fennel, the slow shape

of desire and slick of otter.
    In a place burning with hate

it will heal like clearest water.
    A crowd of clocks clacking together

makes no time but a sound like streams
    where deer drinking conquer the armed man

by their vast astonishment and silence.
    It is a meeting he does not expect.

Who can command this coming?
    Out of the dark rafters, the skeletal shed,

it spreads like a blossoming field, raises
    a field forgotten, forgiving, to quicken and taste.

O see the healing, the linnets, the spinning worm,
    the flash and pivot of creatures living
        under the skin of grace.

from

A New Herball

—————————————————————————

(1968)

Moss

A green sky underfoot:
the skin of moss
holds the footprints of
star-footed birds.

With moss-fingers, with
filigree they line
their nests in the
forks of the trees.

All around, the apples
are falling, the leaves
snap, the sun moves
away from the earth.

Only the moss stays,
decently covers the
roots of things, itself
rooted in silence:

rocks coming alive
underfoot, rain no
man heard fall. Moss,
stand up for us,

the small birds and
the great sun. You know

our trees and apples,
our parrots and women's eyes.

Keep us in your green
body, laid low
and still blossoming
under the snow.

Arbor

As a child she planted
these roses, these vines
heavy with trumpets and honey.

Now at the end of her life
she asks for an arbor. At night
she sees roses rooted in heaven,

wisteria hanging its vineyards
over her head, all green things
climbing, climbing.

She wants to walk through this door,
not as she walks to the next
room but to another place

altogether. She will leave her cane
at the door but the door is
necessary. She knows how the raw

space in a wall nearly burned or
newly born makes children pause
and step in. It leads somewhere.

They look out on another country.

Out of War

In the forest a soldier sees
a child asleep and a fox
rocking the cradle.
The great paws sheathe

blades curved like sickles,
gentle as moths
for rocking. The man waits,
his hand on the new grenades

that he came to throw
in the forest where
no one lives
save a child and a slow

fox with its great claws
curled for catching
small fish and berries
and leaves. They pause,

the fox and his clever
enemy, the man who wants
someone to kill; surely
that would restore whatever

it is he's lost, the weather
of inward mornings, of play
between fox and man's child, of how
they lie down together.

from

19 *Masks for the Naked Poet*

(1971)

for Jerome Badanes (1937–1995)
and Jeriann Hilderley

The Poet Takes a Photograph of His Heart

The doctor told him,
Something is living in your heart.
The poet borrowed a camera.
He told his heart to smile.
He slipped the plate under his ribs
and caught his heart running out of the picture.
He told his heart to relax.
It beat on the plate with its fist.
It did not want to lose its face!
He told his heart he was taking nothing
but an icon by which to remember it.
Then the heart stood up like a bandstand
and the wren who lived under the eaves
left her nest and started
the long journey south.

The Poet Invites the Moon for Supper

Tonight a stranger followed me home.
He wore an overcoat and feathers.
His head was as light as summer.
When I saw how much light he spilled
on the street, I knew he was rich.

He wanted to make me his heir.
I said, no thank you, I have a father.
He wanted to give me the snow to wife.
I said, no thank you, I have a sweetheart.
He wanted to make me immortal.
And I said, no thank you, but when you see
somebody putting me into the mouth
of the earth, don't fret.
I am a song.
Someone is writing me down.
I am disappearing into the ear of a rose.

The Poet Writes Many Letters

Bills for horses he never bought,
an inventory of stars,
a plea for his left leg;
he answers them all
so beautifully that the stableman
saves the letter and hangs it over his bed,
the air saves the invoice and says it aloud,
the one-legged beggar saves his rejection
and eats it with honey.
A hundred years later an Arabian mare
grazing on the steppes of his longing
breaks her own record speed.
A deaf-mute reads his refusal and feels loved.
A one-eyed milkman jogging his horses over the snow
warms his hands at the penitent tongues of stars.

The Poet Enters the Sleep of the Bees

Turning to honey one morning, I passed
through their glass cells and entered
the sleep of the bees.
The bees were making a lexicon
of the six-sided names of God,

clover's breath, dewflesh,
ritual of the thorn, a definitive work
to graft the names to their roots.
For days I hiked over their sleepshod sounds.
At last I saw a green lion
eating a hole in the sun,

and a red dragon burning itself alive
to melt the snow that lay like a cap
on the sleep of the bees.
Their sleep was a factory
of sweetness with no author.

Every syllable was swept clean,
every act was without motive.
Please forgive me this poor translation.
How could I hold
my past to my present when I heard
ten thousand tongues flowing along like gold?

The Poet Turns His Enemy
into a Pair of Wings

His enemy was a dragon laced with medals.
It picked his pockets, hid his poems,
beat its tail on his head at night,
blew the nose off his wife's face.
For God's sake, peace! cried the poet.
Then the dragon jumped on his back.
Warm in his lizardskin coat he stepped outside.
No one, no one else in the snowy city
wore a lizardskin coat.
Its purple hearts jingled like temple bells.
It rested its pointed chin on the poet's head.
Go right, said the dragon.
The poet skipped left.
Go up, said the dragon.
The poet went downtown.
At one o'clock it turned yellow.
At two o'clock it turned green.
Go up, said the dragon, or let me be.
I am Salamander, fireman of the stars,
bound to cross my brow with their ashes.
How shall I go? asked the poet.
Just as you are, said the dragon,
day in night, night in hand,
hand in pocket, pocket in poem,
poem in bone, bone in flesh,
flesh in flight.

The Poet Tracks Down the Moon

In the woods, the old moon is barking
and humming and turning around on her nest.
The poet calls his dogs and carries
a net to catch her, this quartz quail,
this silver truffle slivering into the dark.

When the moon hears him, she turns out her light,
leaves her skin under a bush like patience,
and covers her tracks with a sigh.
To the river she throws the first letter
of her language, the crescent, the open trap.

It stands for *canny* and *clever.* She throws it
like bread to catch the poet who at once
swims into her net. When he walks, the moon
hangs her thin wire around his ankle,
hangs her tiny hook in the gills of his heart.

The Baker's Wife
Tells His Horoscope with Pretzels

At dawn he visits the baker's wife
in her Tenth Street kitchen.
Already the ovens are hot.
Already a bride and groom stand up
on the plain face of heaven.
Already birthdays write themselves
on the chocolate cheeks of the moon.

The baker's wife, powdered with fine stars,
ties back the future with pretzels,
hundreds of pretzels crossing their arms in prayer.

"In the house of the archer I see you
teaching the sun to heel.
Though the moon cancels the sign of the two fish,
though she locks the sun in the house of the crab,
though she draws off the nations in tides of folly,
for you the lamb will lie down with the lion,
the virgin will put her head in your lap."

The Poet Stumbles upon
the Astronomer's Orchards

Once a scholar showed me the sky.
He held up a grapefruit:
here is the sun.
He held up an orange:
this is the harvest moon.
If you watch my hands, you will see
how the sun stays in its socket,
how the earth turns, how the moon
ripens and falls and swells again.

Under an axle tree, I took my seat.
The leaves were stars
juggling pineapples and pears.
                    What a show!
A thousand lemons are rolling through space,
avocados nudge down the rings of Jupiter
and coconuts shake the galaxy to its teeth
till the tree loses its leaves.

But there is a star in my apple when I cut it
and some hungry traveler is paring the moon away.

The Poet's Wife
Watches Him Enter the Eye of the Snow

She knew he was writing a poem
because everything in the room
was slowly sifting away:
her dustpan the color of buttercups,
her eyeglasses and her sink
and her five masks praising the sun.

That night she saw him ascend.
He floated above their bed,
he gathered the dark strands
of the poem like a tide.

On his nose her glasses polished
themselves to crystals. On his back
the dustpan fanned out
like a saffron cape.
Now he was turning his face toward the sun
and riding her simple sink into heaven.

In the morning she calls to the newsboy:
"How can I, wife of the poet,
know what he saw and did there?
It is enough that I open my eyes

and my glasses perch on my nose
and show me the brittle dreams of parrots.
Enough that my dustpan believes it shoulders
the broken bones of those warriors the stars,
that my sink gurgles for joy,
and my five masks tell me more
than I knew when I made them."

from

Carpenter of the Sun

(1974)

For You, Who Didn't Know

At four a.m. I dreamed myself on that beach
where we'll take you after you're born.
I woke in a wave of blood.

Lying in the back seat of a nervous Chevy
I counted the traffic lights, lonely as planets.
Starlings stirred in the robes of Justice

over the Town Hall. Miscarriage of justice,
they sang, while you, my small client,
went curling away like smoke under my ribs.

Kick me! I pleaded. Give me a sign
that you're still there!
Train tracks shook our flesh from our bones.

Behind the hospital rose a tree of heaven.
       You can learn something from everything,
       a rabbi told his Hasidim who did not believe it.

       I didn't believe it, either. O rabbi,
       what did you learn on the train to Belsen?
       That because of one second one can miss everything.

There are rooms on this earth for emergencies.
A sleepy attendant steals my clothes and my name,
and leaves me among the sinks on an altar of fear.

"Your name. Your name. Sign these papers,
    authorizing us in our wisdom to save the child.
    Sign here for circumcision. Your faith, your faith."

O rabbi, what can we learn from the telegraph?
asked the Hasidim, who did not understand.
And he answered, *That every word is counted and charged.*

"This is called a dobtone," smiles the doctor.
He greases my belly, stretched like a drum,
and plants a microphone there, like a flag.

A thousand thumping rabbits! Savages clapping for joy!
A heart dancing its name, I'm-here, I'm-here!
The cries of fishes, of stars, the tunings of hair!

O rabbi, what can we learn from a telephone?
My shiksa daughter, your faith, your faith
that what we say here is heard there.

A Kind of Healing

When I felt you leap, we found you a name.
Though you are all head and belly,
though you have the gills of a fish,
shy and mysterious, you are biding your time.

Though I am a teacher, I can learn plenty from you.
About entrances, for example, and waiting
to show forth at the right time.
"Believe that it grows," I hear myself saying.

"You want to write? You can't name it?
Put it away, let it alone.
Prepare for the coming of ripeness
with songs of Thanksgiving."

O sing unto the Lord a new song.

We are a Christian nation,
we have too many days off for famous men.
Someday I'll tell you how we marched,
you in me, me in forty thousand,

bearing no flags but the names of the dead.
Living and dead leap in the womb of a terrible war.
Once they too lay nameless and waiting,
now they wait and do not cry when we call them.

I carried the name of a boy from Harlem,
Washington Watson, who left no child

and no great works, nothing except his name,
which I called out to the spiked fence

along the avenues of justice and remorse,
in the great roll call of the dead,
as you danced, shameless and merry,
and far away, men gave up their names

faster than any woman could carry them.

Carpenter of the Sun

My child goes forth to fix the sun,
a hammer in his hand and a pocketful of nails.
Nobody else has noticed the crack.

Twilight breaks on the kitchen floor.
His hands clip and hammer the air.
He pulls something out,

something small, like a bad tooth,
and he puts something back,
and the kitchen is full of peace.

All this is done very quietly,
without payment or promises.

In Praise of ABC

In the beginning were the letters,
wooden, awkward, and everywhere.
Before the Word was the slow scrabble of fire and water.

God bless my son and his wooden letters
who has gone to bed with A in his right hand and Z in his left,
who has walked all day with C in his shoe and said nothing,
who has eaten of his napkin the word Birthday,
and who has filled my house with the broken speech of wizards.

To him the grass makes its gentle sign.
For him the worm letters her gospel truth.
To him the pretzel says, I am the occult
descendant of the first blessed bread
and the lost cuneiform of a grain of wheat.

Kneading bread, I found in my kitchen half an O.
Now I wait for someone to come from far off
holding the other half, saying,
What is broken shall be made whole.
Match half for half; now do you know me again?

Thanks be to God for my house seeded with dark sayings
and my rooms rumpled and badly lit
but richly lettered with the secret raisins of truth.

A Humane Society

If they don't take animals,
I cannot possibly stay at the Hilton
no matter how broad the beds
nor how excellent the view.
Not even if the faucets run hot and cold pearls,
not even if the sheets are cloth of gold,

because I never go anywhere without my raccoon,
my blue raccoon in his nifty mask,
the shadow cast by mind over sight.
I never go abroad without consulting his paw
or reading the weather in the whites of his eyes.
I would share my last crust with his wise mouth.

And even if the manager promised
provisions could be made for a blue raccoon,
I cannot possibly stay at the Hyatt,
no matter how many angels feather the fondues,
no matter how many bishops have blessed the soup,
because I never go anywhere without my cat,

my fuchsia cat in her choirboy bow,
in the purity of whose sleep a nun would feel shamed,
in whose dreams the mouse lies down with the elephant.
I never go to bed without setting her at the door
for her sleep robs even the serpent of poison
and no door closes where she takes her rest,

but even if the manager said, very well,
we can accommodate, for a fee, a fuchsia cat,

I cannot possibly stay at the Plaza.
I understand bears are not welcome there.
I understand that everyone walks on two legs,
and I never go anywhere without my bear

who is comelier of gait than any woman,
who wears no shoes and uses no speech
but many a day has laid down his life for me
in this city of purses, assassins, and the poor.
He would give me his coat and walk abroad in his bones,
and he loves a sunny window and a kind face.

I need a simple room papered with voices
and sorrows without circumstance, and an old lady
in the kitchen below who has welcomed
visitors more desperate than ourselves
and who fondly recalls a pregnant woman riding a donkey
and three crazy men whose only map was a star.

Walking Poem

How beautifully the child I carry on my back
teaches me to become a horse.
How quickly I learn to stay
between shafts, blinders, and whips,
bearing the plough

and the wagon loaded with hay,
or to break out of trot and run
till we're flying through cold streams.
He who kicks my commands
knows I am ten times his size

and that I am servant to small hands.
It is in mowed fields I move best,
watching the barn grow toward me,
the child quiet, his sleep piled like hay
on my back as we slip over the dark hill

and I carry the sun away.

Marriage Amulet

You are polishing me like old wood.
At night we curl together like two rings
on a dark hand. After many nights,
the rough edges wear down.

If this is aging, it is warm as fleece.
I will gleam like ancient wood.
I will wax smooth, my crags and cowlicks
well-rubbed to show my grain.

Some sage will keep us in his hand for peace.

How to Stuff a Pepper

Now, said the cook, I will teach you
how to stuff a pepper with rice.

Take your pepper green, and gently,
for peppers are shy. No matter which side
you approach, it's always the backside.
Perched on green buttocks, the pepper sleeps.
In its silk tights, it dreams
of somersaults and parsley,
of the days when the sexes were one.

Slash open the sleeve
as if you were cutting a paper lantern,
and enter a moon, spilled like a melon,
a fever of pearls,
a conversation of glaciers.
It is a temple built to the worship
of morning light.

I have sat under the great globe
of seeds on the roof of that chamber,
too dazzled to gather the taste I came for.
I have taken the pepper in hand,
smooth and blind, a runt in the rich
evolution of roses and ferns.
You say I have not yet taught you

to stuff a pepper?
Cooking takes time.

Next time we'll consider the rice.

Roots

This squash is my good cousin,
says the vegetable man,
rolling his pushcart through November.

These parsnips are first class.
I recommend with my whole heart.
I know the family.

Believe me, lady, I know
what I'm talking.
And I give you a good price.

I throw in the carrots free.
Carrots like this you got?
So what you want?

I wrap in the best Yiddish newspaper.
A dollar a year. Takes me
ten minutes to read it,

an hour to read the English.
Potatoes you need, maybe?
My wife says I eat too many

potatoes. In Poland, in war,
we ate potatoes, soup,
baked, boiled.

All my family was ploughed under
except me. So what can I say
to someone that he don't like

potatoes? Positively last chance,
because tomorrow it might snow.
In winter I don't come.

Look for me when the snow goes,
and if I don't come back,
think that I moved, maybe.

I'm eighty-two already,
and what is Paradise
without such potatoes?

A Psalm for Running Water

Running water, you are remembered and called.
Physician of clover and souls; hock, glove
and slipper of stones.

Stitch thyme and buttercup to my boots.
Make me tread the psalm and sign of water
falling, when I am going the other way,
climbing the mountain for a clear view of home.

After winter's weeding and the fire's gap in the woods,
first ferns, trillium, watercress,
this vivid text, Water, shows your hand.

The trees stand so spare a child may write them.
You, Water, sing them like an old score,
settled, pitched soft and fresh,
and wash our wounds when we fall.

A hundred Baptists, hand in hand,
rise and fall in your body and rise again,
praising the Lord, whose hand, I think, wears you.

For all this and more, my grandmother
thumped out of bed on Easter and tramped
over gorse and thorn and wild thistle
to the water smiling through her husband's field.

She capped some in a cruet;
    the wink of God,
    the quick motion of ourselves in time,
    flashing! flashing!

In Praise of Unwashed Feet

Because I can walk over hot coals,
because I can make doctors turn green
and shoe salesmen avert their eyes,
because I have added yet another use
to the hundred and one uses of Old Dutch Cleanser;
because they tell me the secrets of miners and small boys,
because they keep me in good standing and continual grace
in the ashes and dust of the last rites,
because they carry my great bulk without complaint,
because they don't smell;
because it's taken me years
to grow my own shoes, like the quaint signatures of truth,
because they are hard and gentle as lion's pads,
pard's paw, mule's hoof and cock's toes,
because they can't make poems or arguments
but speak in an aching tongue or not at all
and come home at night encrusted with stones,
calluses, grass, all that the head forgets
        and the foot knows.

The Animals Welcome Persephone

Coming from the white fields
she will at first see nothing.

They know this and they wait,
the hedgehog, the owl, the mole,

at the mouth of the cave
watching the young queen.

She is saying goodbye to her
mother. She thinks it is

forever. The animals know this;
the owl has sat at many a deathbed.

Only man thinks he can live
forever. Now the air

withers with cold. Behind her,
leaves snap and go under.

By the mineral light of a worm's
eye, the bear's coat shines,

the fish under the earth surface
like diamonds. All who have fed

on the sun come forward,
showing how each nerve

beats with it still, how her death
is not the darkness she fears.

They carry their own stars to the dead.

When There Were Trees

I can remember when there were trees,
great tribes of spruces who deckled themselves in light,
beeches buckled in pewter, meeting like Quakers,
the golden birch, all cutwork satin,
courtesan of the mountains; the paper birch
trying all summer to take off its clothes
like the swaddlings of the newborn.

The hands of a sassafras blessed me.
I saw maples fanning the fire in their stars,
heard the coins of the aspens rattling like teeth,
saw cherry trees spraying fountains of light,
smelled the wine my heel pressed from ripe apples,
saw a thousand planets bobbing like bells
on the sleeve of the sycamore, chestnut, and lime.

The ancients knew that a tree is worthy of worship.
A few wise men from their tribes broke through the sky,
climbing past worlds to come and the rising moon
on the patient body of the tree of life,
and brought back the souls of the newly slain,
no bigger than apples, and dressed the tree
as one of themselves and danced.

Even the conquerors of this country
lifted their eyes and found the trees
more comely than gold: *Bright green trees,*
the whole land so green it is pleasure to look on it,

and the greatest wonder to see the diversity.
During that time, I walked among trees,
the most beautiful things I had ever seen.*

Watching the shadows of trees, I made peace with mine.
Their forked darkness gave motion to morning light.
Every night the world fell to the shadows,
and every morning came home, the dogwood floating
its petals like moons on a river of air,
the oak kneeling in wood sorrel and fern,
the willow washing its hair in the stream.

And I saw how the logs from the mill floated
downstream, saw otters and turtles that rode them,
and though I heard the saws whine in the woods
I never thought men were stronger than trees.
I never thought those tribes would join
the buffalo and the whale, the leopard, the seal, the wolf,
and the folk of this country who knew how to sing them.

Nothing I ever saw washed off the sins of the world
so well as the first snow dropping on trees.
We shoveled the pond clear and skated under their branches,

> **Adapted from the journals of Christopher Columbus, as rendered in William Carlos Williams's* In the American Grain.

our voices muffled in their huge silence.
The trees were always listening to something else.
They didn't hear the beetle with the hollow tooth
grubbing for riches, gnawing for empires, for gold.

Already the trees are a myth,
half gods, half giants in whom nobody believes.
But I am the oldest woman on earth,
and I can remember when there were trees.

What the Grass Said

All summer the trees are packing to go.
They engrave their maps on their hands.
They have thousands of hands
and no two maps are the same.

The further they travel, the less they move.
Traveling for them is throwing the maps away,
one by one till they stand naked.
You can see the sunlight through their ribs.

They don't forget to put out buds before they go,
but even that is a way of saying goodbye,
got to make a new map out of my blood,
got to find my home on the mountain.

Clearing the Air

It's been years since you tried to kill me.
Biking home one night, I saw only your legs
stepping behind a tree, then you fell on my throat
like a cat. My books crashed the birds out of sleep.
We rolled in the leaves like lovers. My eyes popped
like Christmas lights, veins snapped, your teeth wore

my blood, your fingers left bars on my neck.
I can't remember your name,
and I saw your face only in court.
You sat in a box, docile as old shoes.
And I, who had never felt any man's weight
sometimes felt yours for nights afterwards.

Well, I'm ready to forgive
and I don't want to forget.
Sometimes I tell myself that we met
differently, on a train. You give me
a Batman comic and show me your passport.
I have nothing but my report card,

but I offer my mother's fudge for the grapes
rotting the one paper bag you carry.
In my tale you are younger and loved.
Outside you live in a thousand faces
and so do your judges, napping in parks,
rushing to fires, folded like bats on the truck,

mad and nude in a white Rolls
pinching dollars and leather behinds.
Burned from a tree by your betters, you take
to the streets and hang in the dark like a star,
making me see your side, waking me
with the blows and the weight of it.

from

Household Tales of Moon and Water

(*1982*)

Questions My Son Asked Me,
Answers I Never Gave Him

1. Do gorillas have birthdays?
   Yes. Like the rainbow, they happen.
   Like the air, they are not observed.

2. Do butterflies make a noise?
   The wire in the butterfly's tongue
   hums gold.
   Some men hear butterflies
   even in winter.

3. Are they part of our family?
   They forgot us, who forgot how to fly.

4. Who tied my navel? Did God tie it?
   God made the thread: O man, live forever!
   Man made the knot: enough is enough.

5. If I drop my tooth in the telephone
   will it go through the wires and bite someone's ear?
   I have seen earlobes pierced by a tooth of steel.
   It loves what lasts.
   It does not love flesh.
   It leaves a ring of gold in the wound.

6. If I stand on my head
   will the sleep in my eye roll up into my head?
   Does the dream know its own father?
   Can bread go back to the field of its birth?

7. Can I eat a star?
   Yes, with the mouth of time
   that enjoys everything.

8. Could we Xerox the moon?
   This is the first commandment:

   I am the moon, thy moon.
   Thou shalt have no other moons before thee.

9. Who invented water?
   The hands of the air, that wanted to wash each other.

10. What happens at the end of numbers?
    I see three men running toward a field.
    At the edge of the tall grass, they turn into light.

11. Do the years ever run out?
    God said, I will break time's heart.
    Time ran down like an old phonograph.
    It lay flat as a carpet.
    At rest on its threads, I am learning to fly.

Night Light

The moon is not green cheese.
It is china and stands in this room.
It has a ten-watt bulb and a motto:
Made in Japan.

Whey-faced, doll-faced,
it's closed as a tooth
and cold as the dead are cold
till I touch the switch.

Then the moon performs
its one trick:
it turns into a banana.
It warms to its subjects,

it draws us into its light,
just as I knew it would
when I gave ten dollars
to the pale clerk

in the store that sold
everything.
She asked, did I have a car?
She shrouded the moon in tissue

and laid it to rest in a box.
The box did not say *Moon.*
It said *This side up.*
I tucked the moon into my basket

and bicycled into the world.
By the light of the sun

I could not see the
moon under my sack of apples,

moon under slab of salmon,
moon under clean laundry,
under milk its sister
and bread its brother,

moon under meat.
Now supper is eaten.
Now laundry is folded away.
I shake out the old comforters.

My nine cats find their places
and go on dreaming where they left off.
My son snuggles under the heap.
His father loses his way in a book.

It is time to turn on the moon.
It is time to live by a different light.

Angels in Winter

Mercy is whiter than laundry,
great baskets of it, piled like snowmen.
In the cellar I fold and sort and watch
through a squint in the dirty window
the plain bright snow.

Unlike the earth, snow is neuter.
Unlike the moon, it stays.
It falls, not from grace, but a silence
which nourishes crystals.
My son catches them on his tongue.

Whatever I try to hold perishes.
My son and I lie down in white pastures
of snow and flap like the last survivors
of a species that couldn't adapt to the air.
Jumping free, we look back at

angels, blurred fossils of majesty and justice
from the time when a ladder of angels
joined the house of the snow
to the houses of those whom it covered
with a dangerous blanket or a healing sleep.

As I lift my body from the angel's,
I remember the mad preacher of Indiana
who chose for the site of his kingdom
the footprint of an angel and named the place
New Harmony. Nothing of it survives.

The angels do not look back
to see how their passing changes the earth,
the way I do, watching the snow,

and the waffles our boots print on its unleavened face,
and the nervous alphabet of the pheasant's feet,

and the five-petaled footprint of the cat,
and the shape of snowshoes, white and expensive as tennis,
and the deep ribbons tied and untied by sleds.
I remember the millions who left the earth;
it holds no trace of them,

as it holds of us, tracking through snow,
so tame and defenseless
even the air could kill us.

Two Roman Goddesses

First goddess: Deverra

The string broke.
The beads scattered.
I could never collect my wits
if not for you, Deverra,

inventor of brooms.
What worries my feet
is brushed aside.

By moonlight I make
a clean sweep;
ten blue beads,
two pennies,

and a silver pin.
"There is great luck in pins,"
says my mother,

an honest woman
who never lets a pin lie,
not even a crooked one.
"Sweep dust out the door

and you lose your luck,"
says my grandmother,
the unconsecrated Bishop of Dust

and Adviser to Ashes,
herding the lowly together
from dust to dust.
"Don't throw yourself away

on the first man that asks you."
Outside, rain glistens.
I am patient as cats' tongues.

By moonlight I take stock.
Kneeling in dust
at this miniature market,
I pick and choose.

What is lost to sight
is not lost, says the moon,
rinsed clear

as if my mother
rode her broom over it,
lifting the clouds
and letting down

columns of moonlight.
A little temple.
A little night music.

Second goddess: Juno Lucina

By moonlight I see
the anger of shoes,
their laces clenched into knots.

I take the shoes in my lap.
I loosen their tongues.
I take both sides

of the quarrel:
left strand,
right strand.

"When you were born," says my mother,
"the midwife untied
shoes, curtains,

everything."
Nevertheless, I came
with the cord round my neck,

tied like a dog
to my mother's darkness.
The goddess found me.

Her left hand carried the moon,
her right hand lay open like a flower,
empty. Feet first, I followed.

The midwife knocked
breath into me
and knotted that cord for good.

Hush, said the goddess.
Your mother's calling.
You can make it alone now.

Lightness Remembered

Nor do these heads sing,
though our breath pushes
a blizzard of glass grapes
through the female wand,

a ring of red plastic,
the better
to blow bubbles with.
Through a bowl of soap soup,

the melts of moonlight,
the seduction of sherbet,
my son draws the wand,
and now in the ring shines

a lens
on which he blows
as if he would clean it,
the better to see

the wind with.
O breath, lovely
shaper that makes
a silken windsock,

a nervous tunnel,
a sack soft enough
to hold the unborn,
a glass egg that breaks free

and floats like a planet
over the rose bush,
casting
its rainbow-lipped
shadow on leaves,
on stones—
O wet nose of a spirit,
cold cheek of

the apples of the air,
though he waves the wand,
though he fans you awake,
though you rise again,

there's no saving you.

How the Hen Sold Her Eggs
to the Stingy Priest

An egg is a grand thing for a journey.

It will make you a small meal on the road
and a shape most serviceable to the hand

for darning socks, and for barter
a purse of gold opens doors anywhere.

If I wished for a world better than this one
I would keep, in an egg till it was wanted,

the gold earth floating on a clear sea.
If I wished for an angel, that would be my way,

the wings in gold waiting to wake,
the feet in gold waiting to walk,

and the heart that no one believed in
beating and beating the gold alive.

Saint Pumpkin

Somebody's in there.
Somebody's sealed himself up
in this round room,
this hassock upholstered in rind,
this padded cell.
He believes if nothing unbinds him
he'll live forever.

Like our first room
it is dark and crowded.
Hunger knows no tongue
to tell it.
Water is glad there.
In this room with two navels
somebody wants to be born again.

So I unlock the pumpkin.
I carve out the lid
from which the stem raises
a dry handle on a damp world.
Lifting, I pull away
wet webs, vines on which hang
the flat tears of the pumpkin,

like fingernails or the currency
of bats. How the seeds shine,
as if water had put out
hundreds of lanterns.
Hundreds of eyes in the windless wood

gaze peacefully past me,
hacking the thickets,

and now a white dew beads the blade.
Has the saint surrendered
himself to his beard?
Has his beard taken root in his cell?

Saint Pumpkin, pray for me,
because when I looked for you, I found nothing,
because unsealed and unkempt, your tomb rots,
because I gave you a false face
and a light of my own making.

The Sleep of the Painted Ladies

This is my task: to move five cocoons
from an old jam jar to the butterfly cage.

Now they sway from the lid—
five corpses on a gallows

that drop their skins, shrunken to commas
and mark the leaf of their last meal.

I should knock before entering.
This is an ancient place

made for nothing but spinning
and falling asleep.

If I were smaller
or the room larger

I would see an old woman
draw from her outlawed wheel

my hundred years' sleep.
I would hear the snapping of threads,

their cry untuned
at the instant of breaking.

Here lies sleep, sheathed in five copper bullets
I can hold in my hand like aspirin,

five painted ladies who wanted
to travel, to forget everything.

The Five Versions of the Icicle

They are the sun's wet nurse, said the mother,
and it milks them to nothing.

They are stockings, said the laundress,
and grievously shrunken.

They are noodles in a broth of diamonds, said the cook,
and they are sausages oiled with light.

They are the parsnips of heaven, said the gardener,
that cannot be grown out of season.

They are the urns of grief, said the widow.
They live on their own tears.

Family Picnic with Wine and Water

On the banks of a stream,
a Man and a Woman unfold a cloth.

She sets out three goblets
and he sets out a bottle of Saint Père.

She sets out three plates
and he sets the newspaper over his face.

Below the banks where roots
muscle into the water

somebody crouches, half-naked,
picking up pebbles, reading them,

tossing them back to the stream,
somebody small and glad,

the Finder,
the Shining One.

Two Allegorical Figures

Lady, haven't we met before?
Aren't you the baker?
Didn't you take me into your kitchen

and gather the slow sad dough,
too stupid even to breathe,
into white hills, coffins, and domes?

It was you who bustled them into the dark
ovens of great change.
It was I who clapped for the sleepers

vested in crusts of gold,
yet private as beehives and spare
as a hermit's hut.

And that gentleman out in the yard,
the chairman of sacrifice,
he who breaks in horses and doors to rooms

we would never leave if he didn't
carry the walls away: it was he
who broke bread, still warm,

the butter undone at one stroke,
the mild flesh coming alive in our mouths,
honored at last in its own kingdom.

Country Scene

At the desk of the Lamb and Flag sits a Great Dane,
his paw grazing the bell we must touch to wake him.
He shakes himself, he jangles the coins on his neck.
We have arrived at midnight without reservations,
father, mother, son. Even our fear is asleep.

His peaked ears twitch as they gather our names.
For a long time he studies the black book
of all who have certainly stayed and all who might.
Then he asks us in low tones, why have we come?
Did the cock in the kettle crow?

Did a donkey sing?
We shake our heads. No, we heard nothing like that.
In the clock behind him, a sun is rising
like a burnished peach on a perfectly painted tree.
Behind the sun a rabbit is running away,

and behind the rabbit a pack of hounds
flushes the hours out. Eleven! Twelve!
Time passes, stately as deer on the mountain.
The Great Dane listens for yet one more.
But nothing appears, nothing has changed at all.

He waves us to follow him, he has a room that will do,
and he gives us a key fit to open nothing.
It is dotted and crossed, and solid silver.
It waits on my palm like a word
that would light this whole house

if I knew how to say it.

My Life on the Road
with Bread and Water

*There was once a woman who loved
a river.*
—African folk tale

In Which I Meet Bread and Catch Water

I said to BREAD,
Give me something to catch WATER,
a gift that will give him to me forever.

Bread looked into my head
and said Table.
I went home and made Table.
Water set Table,
Water ate his supper,
folded his napkin and went away.

To Bread I said,
Table is useful
but not necessary.

Bread looked into my head
and said Chair.
I went home and made Chair.
Water sat down,
Water stood up,
put out his cigarette and went away.

To Bread I said,
Chair is kind
but not affectionate.

Bread looked into my head
and said Tree.
I went home and made Tree.

Much followed from the making of Tree,
such as roots, bluets,
boars, blue jays, beetles,
worms, etc.
Water lay down in the shade
and later, much later,

chopped down Tree,
burned it all winter
and went away.

To Bread I said,
Tree is patient
but not prudent.

Then Bread looked into my head
and saw emptiness and enormous light.
He breathed on that light
and wrote on that breath: Mirror.

So I went home and made Mirror.
I made this poem, to hold Water.
Who looks for himself will not find it,
and who sees himself will never know who he sees.

In Which Water Gathers the Full Moon

The hands of Water are milk
freckled with stars.

What loves to touch the
wet feet of the mint
does not make houses or
money.

The moon, small enough to spend,
lies on his open palm.
His fingers close over her,
breaking her shell, snap!

When they open, so still, so still,
the moon remembers herself in time.
There she lies, good as new,
sentimental, absurd,

her white heart pulsing
in the terrible hand of Water.

In Which Water Gives Me the Book of My Ancestors

Water gave me this book.
It is not written for me.
It is written for birds,

snakes, fishes.
See their bones printed
on limestone.

See this track scratched
on the fresh page of the snow,
leading me into the story.

Someone has gone before me,
cutting the leaves, and now and then
marking a useful passage.

In Which Water Turns Himself into a Feast

Water says: Come to the feast,
and he puts up his banks,
his mud, his black willows,
his sleek rushes.

Mud says: Stop here.
His ways are not your ways.
If he opens his gate,
it is not for you.

Bread, rabbits, stars,
ribbons, lamentations,
all surge forward.
Who is in charge here?

Are we birds
that he feeds us by hand?
or beggars that we
open our fists to be fed?

I wanted something I could carry away,
not this giving which vanishes,

not this quickening
which belongs to no one.

In Which I Leave Water and Find Road

When I enter your house, I bow my head
because even my Lord Fire attends you.
For you, candles lower their mild eyes.
When I sit at your table, I speak with Fire.
I speak of the fire of my youth.
May it burn like a star in my age.
I invoke his heat against winter,
cold feet, and a cold heart.
O, in your service, how the gloss
has gone off him!

Rising to go, I give you my hands
to keep, to remember me by.
You shake your head, *No, no.*
You are too kind.
In my left hand you put
a flagon of ice
and in my right the measure
of bread which you baked
for me in the ashes of morning,
for the long journey away from you.

Blessing for Letting Go

I pick up Sad,
I burn it, I scatter the ashes.

Now be thou glad.
Go not with any other woman.
Be curious.
Be beautiful.
Shine.
Life of the earth,
protect this one
who is going to meet you.

from

The Ballad of Biddy Early

(1987)

The Ballad of Biddy Early

"I've an empty stomach,
  you've an empty purse.
  You feel your fingers freezing?
  Outside it's ten times worse,
  so listen to my story.
  Forget the wind and rain.
  It's time for bed," the tinker said,
"but pass the cup again.

"I sing of Biddy Early,
  the wise woman of Clare.
  Many's the man admires her
  carrot-colored hair,
  and many those that come to her
  on horseback or by cart,
  for she can heal a broken leg
  or a broken heart.

"She keeps a magic bottle
  in whose majestic eye
  a tiny coffin twinkles
  and if it sinks, you die.
  It rises, you grow better
  and slip out of your pain.
  It's time for bed," the tinker said,
"but pass the cup again.

"She covers the great bottle
  and runs to fetch the small,
  filled with a bright elixir,

honey and sage and gall.
She'll take no gold or silver
but maybe a speckled hen.
It's time for bed," the tinker said.
"Let's pass the cup again.

"*Follow the stream, she told me.*
Go where the salmon goes.
Avoid mischievous bridges
for even water knows
if you should drop this bottle—"
He turned and spoke no more.
Biddy Early's shadow
was listening at the door.

How the Magic Bottle Gave Biddy Its Blessing

"Sighing stones, ghosts and bones,
  and who will dig a grave
  for roaring Tom, that bloody man
  who with a pistol gave
  death to seven people?
  The gravediggers have fled.
  So let the lightning bury him,"
  the deathwatch beetle said.

"Even the wicked need a grave
  and it's a dreadful thing
  for any man to make his bed
  under the vulture's wing.
  Give me the spade and pickax.
  A murderer who's dead
  can do no harm to anyone,"
  Biddy Early said.

She sank her spade into the sod—
  the stones began to weep.
"The little mice," said Biddy,
"are singing in their sleep."
  She sank her spade into the roots—
  their cry turned her to ice.
  The deathwatch beetle snickered,
"An owl has caught the mice."

Six feet down in darkness
  she heard the shovel chime

against an old blue bottle
glittering under grime.
With sleeve and spit she polished it
and heard the bottle call,
"Of all things born at midnight
I am most magical.

"Nothing known shall come to pass,
no secret word or wish,
that I have not reflected.
Bird, beast, or fish,
every living thing shall praise
the healing in your hand,
Biddy, the bravest woman
in all of Ireland."

Charm of the Gold Road,
the Silver Road,
and the Hidden Road

On my thumb
I spun
two roads
from one thread,
half silver,
half gold.
I made them
and laid them
over the land
and said,

"May those who follow you
find gold but not glowworms,
coins but not crickets,
treasure but not tree toads,
silver but not silence,
money but not moonlight,
                    not magic,

                    and not me."

How the Queen of the Gypsies
Met Trouble-and-Pain

My name is Maureen, I'm the tinker-town queen.
My caravan travels from Gort to Kildare.
When my pony went lame, I remembered the fame
of Biddy the healer, wise woman of Clare.
Bright star of the morning, she gave me fair warning:
"Under my bridge huddles Trouble-and-Pain.
For the sake of this bottle, the creature will throttle
both you and your horse as you cross its domain."

I gave her a ring, hammered out like a wing,
I gave her green ribbons to tie up her hair,
a velveteen fan and a new frying pan,
and I left with her blessing for Limerick Fair.
When we came to the bridge, my horse wouldn't budge.
The bottle grew frightened, it trembled and sighed,
and the harder I held it, the stronger I felt it:
a ghostly hand grappled, a ghostly mouth cried,

"May your horse never walk, may your son never talk.
May the saber-toothed gnats make a nest in your hair.
May your logs never burn, may your dog never learn,
and your purse turn to feathers at Limerick Fair.
May your buttermilk bark, may your lanterns go dark,

and your skillets and petticoats take to the air.
May you drown in the lake, unless I can take
that bottle of Biddy's, wise woman of Clare."

When it reared up its head, I took courage and said,
"By my mother's gold tooth and my father's glass eye—"
Then down the bridge clattered, the bottle was shattered,
but Trouble-and-Pain was more frightened than I.
Some say life is brief as the fall of a leaf,
and nothing lives long that lives under the sun,
but friends and relations in five gypsy nations
shall whisper my story till stories are done.

How Biddy Called Back Friday, Her Lost Pig

Friday, my lost pig, come and find me now.
May the thief that took you be a stone on Wednesday.
May the pen that keeps you be a road on Thursday.
May the rope that binds you run away on Friday.
On Friday, on Friday.
Day of the west wind on the nine fields,
Day to milk the eight cows of patience,
Day to crack the seven walnuts of wisdom,
Day to feed the six salmons of truth,
Day to bake you five loaves of bread,
Day to take your fear from the knife,
Day of acorns, day of sweet mud, day to open all gates
for my lost pig, my delight, my Friday.

Biddy Early Makes a Long Story Short

I, Biddy Early, come from the Red Hills.
My mother traveled under the cold sky
and carried me, her firstborn, on her back.
May the roads she walked stay with me till I die.

I am at home with hunger. For my bread
I learned to haul stones, scrub floors, and cook.
When Mother died, a wren taught me to read
the spells in streams and stones. Earth was my book.

The priest tells me, "Biddy, come to Mass."
I say, "Father, when I kneel down alone
the people whisper things. I want to live
out of their sight, with crickets and cats and stones,

"and when I die, I shall give back to Earth
all her gifts for the healing of hurts and ills.
I shall come back in water and words and leaves,
I, Biddy Early, asleep in the Red Hills."

Song from the Far Side of Sleep

Lullaby, my little cat,
Lord of Mouse and Knave of Bat.
Hail, Mischief, full of grace,
who did lately love this place.

Lullaby your crescent claws
in the chambers of your paws,
which you sharpen day and night,
keeping all my kettles bright.

Lullaby your gentle purr.
What small spirits did you lure
to the mushroom rings I made
and the lesser spells we laid?

Lullaby your pebbled tongue.
Keep my velvets ever young.
Keep my slippers ever slick
with the patience of a lick.

Lullaby your lively tail.
Never have I seen it fail,
spirits gone and revels done,
to point the quickest highway home.

Eternal life, eternal death
hang on our Creator's breath.
Little tiger in God's eye,
remember Biddy's lullaby.

from

Water Walker

(1989)

A Wreath to the Fish

Who is this fish, still wearing its wealth,
flat on my drainboard, dead asleep,
its suit of mail proof only against the stream?
What is it to live in a stream,
to dwell forever in a tunnel of cold,
never to leave your shining birthsuit,
never to spend your inheritance of thin coins?
And who is the stream, who lolls all day
in an unmade bed, living on nothing but weather,
singing, a little mad in the head,
opening her apron to shells, carcasses, crabs,
eyeglasses, the lines of fishermen begging for
news from the interior—oh, who are these lines
that link a big sky to a small stream
and go down for great things:
the cold muscle of the trout,
the shining scrawl of the eel in a difficult passage,
hooked—but who is this hook, this cunning
and faithful fanatic who will not let go
but holds the false bait and the true worm alike
and tears the fish, yet gives it up to the basket
in which it will ride to the kitchen
of someone important, perhaps the Pope
who rejoices that his cook has found such a fish
and blesses it and eats it and rises, saying,
"Children, what is it to live in the stream,
day after day, and come at last to the table,
transfigured with spices and herbs,
a little martyr, a little miracle;
children, children, who is this fish?"

The Feast of St. Tortoise

The day of her wedding, she crouches in the kitchen
and talks to the tortoise. He is older than she,
one of the family but celibate, reserved,

having taken holy orders in chapels of damp earth.
She admires his head, speckled with ivory coins.

She touches his cowl, tender as chamois.
She praises his toadstool legs, his decisive beak,

and the raised ornament of his kindness
as he offers himself for a table

or a gameboard of fretted lacquer:
each hexagon fences a mound

into which a star has fallen so deeply
the whole field is on fire.

Let no guest go hungry.
She sets out a plate of lettuce chopped

into ruffles, the cool cheek
of an apple parceled and peeled.

This is for you, old friend.
He flippers forth. The bright worm of his tail
wags after him.

Psalm to the Newt

Look at the newt. He is worth watching.
The small stars of his hands sign the water.
His fingers thread beads of water on strands of water.

On the canopy of seaweed, he knits his proverbs:
Behold the newt—a weak arm may stir great secrets.
His arms, thin as threads, part curtains of water.
He is a rock to the snail and a snare to the worm.

His back raises an island: sad, a used tire.
The grainy dark of his skin glistens.
To the snails he brings the wet bark of trees.

Old shovel-head, guardian of patience,
you break through the silver roof
of the parliament of water
in the tiny pond of the aquarium.

You who sharpen your tail on the sunrise,
in your livery of cold flames you greet us,
in your vest buttoned with embers you greet us.

You turn on us, slowly, your hooded eyes.
Are you trying to change into something else
or change us into clouds,
shadowy behind glass as the lost gods?

Airport Lobsters

Thrown together in a tank, a litter of lobsters
looks for the way back. When I hurry past, they wave
their taped claws—discreet, like the beaks of birds—
as if I were a door through which they could pass

to deep water, taking their leave of Atlantic shrimp in tins,
smoked oysters, caviar from the Caspian Sea.
My flight is late, and theirs will never arrive.
Their jet eyes pin regret on a watery map.

Moonstalkers, tidekeepers, robots of deep currents,
in whom indigo deepens to midnight when you give up
the ghost, forgive me. I won't forget the shoals of you,
the scrabbling heaps, the sick adrift, light lapping the dead

like a field of samurai in full armor,
your greaves freckled with ashes,
your corselets plated with moonlight,
your antennae still whipping

bubbles of pumped air.

Life at Sea: The Naming of Fish

Stand among fish and admire the angels,
the *Marble Angel,* like grillwork on a sad house
sunk in the suburbs of New Orleans,
and the *Black Angel,* little undertaker of the waters,
and the *Gold Angel,* new-minted, and the *Silver Angel*

that tumbles from God's purse and hides
Silver Dollars in the pockets of water,
their eyes in love with the shyness of pearls.
Schooled in silence, the catfish do not consider
you. *Glass Cats, Green Cats:* whiskered gentlemen,

they paddle to their clubs
in small expensive suits of woven jade.
The *Gold Convict* does not take flight,
though like a note in a bottle
it has lived its pale life in hiding.

What do we know of their risings and settings?
The *Red Oscar* wears twilight.
The *Black Lyre Tail* heads north,
a velvet arrow, happily cutting the waves.
In the last tank, the *Blue Betta*

unfurls his fins, his silk bathrobe.
Like a lively invalid, he admires the tassels,
puts it on, takes it off, on, off,

and glides among branches of hornwort
under the mauve leaves of the purple krinkle.

He does not close his eyes when the sun falls,
slow as a snail through the sky, and new moons
and old moons wish on the *Moon Platys,*
and the stars show us something familiar:
archer, lyre, hunter, dipper, fish.

Poem Made of Water

Praise to my text, Water, which taught me writing,
and praise to the five keepers of the text,
water in Ocean, water in River, water in Lake,
water in cupped hands, water in Tears. Praise
for River, who says: Travel to the source,
poling your raft of words, mindful of currents,
avoiding confusion, delighting in danger
when its spines sparkle, yet keeping
your craft upright, your sentence alive.
You have been sentenced to life.

Praise for Ocean and her generous lesson,
that a great poem changes from generation to generation,
that any reader may find his treasure there
and even the landlocked heart wants to travel.
Praise for that heart, for its tides,
for tiny pools winking in rocks
like poems which make much of small matters:
five snails, two limpets, a closely watched
minnow, his spine a zipper,
and a white stone wearing the handprints of dead coral.

Praise for Tears, which are faithful to grief
not by urns but by understatement.
Praise for thirst, for order in the eye and in the ear
and in the heart, and for water in cupped hands,

for the poem that slakes thirst
and the poem that wakes it.
Praise for Lake, which bustles with swimmers at noon.
I have been one, busy under the light,
piling rocks into castles, not seeing
my work under the ruffled water.

And later—the lake still sleepy in the last light—
the castle squats like the rough draft of a prayer,
disguised as a castle, which tells me
to peer into the dark and interpret shapes in the ooze:
the rowboat rising like a beak, the oil drum rusting,
the pop bottles fisted in weeds, every sunken
thing still, without purpose, dreamed over
till the fisherman's net brings up—
what? a bronze mask? a torso of softest marble?

Go deep. Save, sift, pack, lose, find again.
Come back as snow, rain, tears, crest and foam.
Come back to baptize, heal, drown.
Come back as Water. Come back as Poem.

A Hardware Store
as Proof of the Existence of God

I praise the brightness of hammers pointing east
like the steel woodpeckers of the future,
and dozens of hinges opening brass wings,
and six new rakes shyly fanning their toes,
and bins of hooks glittering into bees,

and a rack of wrenches like the long bones of horses,
and mailboxes sowing rows of silver chapels,
and a company of plungers waiting for God
to claim their thin legs in their big shoes
and put them on and walk away laughing.

In a world not perfect but not bad either
let there be glue, glaze, gum, and grabs,
caulk also, and hooks, shackles, cables, and slips,
and signs so spare a child may read them,
Men, Women, In, Out, No Parking, Beware the Dog.

In the right hands, they can work wonders.

Missionaries Among the Heathen

Elder Wakefield regrets his Walkman
which the stewardess has taken away; is it still
in the bag that did not fit under the seat?
Will it arrive when he does?

Elder Bullock studies French. Elder Smith
sleeps his way into childhood.
Was he twenty when he sat down? His face
relaxes, he is nine, it is the time of crickets,

of gulls wheeling over bunchgrass and sage,
of the thrilling stillness of snakes,
of his father blowing the coals to full flame
on the new barbecue under the heavenly steaks

from the shopping malls of the blessed
where everyone is blond, one way or another.
A voice in the sky says, "We are flying
over Kansas. It is three o'clock in New York
and raining . . ." Elder Bullock twists

the delicate stem of his watch and remembers
the real time: twelve o'clock in Salt Lake City.
The kind lady presents Elder Smith with a tray.
Though he says grace, the food looks no better.

The lettuce does not rise to the occasion.
In the plastic tray a tiny corral
keeps a dead hamburger from flying home to God.
Ah, the sad peas, the grains of rice

that might have been laid by anemic ants.
Ah, the shining pastures of salt,
the fields already white for harvest,
and so many reaping what they did not sow.
Over Chicago he bows his head.

Beyond the window, ghostly beasts float
on plains of glass. Above Newark
they darken. Above Providence they weep
themselves into weather. What is the real time?

He takes the word of God
from its expensive leather case.

Memorial Day in Union City, Michigan

At noon an angel was seen in my grandmother's kitchen,
seen by Maria M———, of sound mind, clear sight.
Hulling the strawberries, tossing their crowns to the sink,
she felt "eyes on me, watching," and turned. Its gaze
rested on the turkey—bare-chested under the basting,
wings lacquered with butter and sharp as elbows—
as if it wondered how birds allow themselves to be caught.

At one o'clock, in the front bedroom, the angel appeared
to my grandmother. She had just lain down for a nap.
"Unwary, like those extinct birds you read about,
who gave their killers a kind of welcome."
It looked in the dresser mirror a long time,
astonished at what it found, another room,
another grandmother, another angel.

At three o'clock the gardener saw a figure
standing on top of the compost and found himself
filled with such longing for another time and condition
he burst into tears. "I thought it was a sleepwalker."
He followed it to the forsythia, lost it to silence
and yellow bells. All afternoon, spading the new plot,
he felt as if he were digging his own grave.

From four till ten, the angel was not seen at all,
but for once in our world, everybody was happy.
I was six years old and no one called me for bed.
My deaf cat purred and purred by my dark window.
In the happy silence of a parade departed,
the forgotten dead accepted our forgiveness,
still air throbbing, distant pulse of a drum.

Science Fiction

Here, said the spirit,
is the Diamond Planet:
Shall I change you into a diamond?
No? Then let us proceed
to the Red Planet,
desert star,
rocks too young to know
lichens. There's plenty
of room. Stay as long
as you like. You don't like?
Then let us go forth to
the Planet of Mists,
the veiled bride,
the pleasures of losing and finding,
the refinement of symbols.
She's all yours.

I see you looking at that blue planet.
It's mostly water.
The land's crowded with
creatures. You have mists
but they rain, diamonds
but they cost. You have
only one moon.
You have camels and babies and cigars
but everything grows up
or wears out.
And on clear nights
you have the stars
without having them.

Coming to the Depot

They are just married, and is he surprised,
he who rode this train with one bag and a beer
and silence when he wanted it and his own speech.

He stares at his wife.
Where did all these bags come from?
What's in them? She is taking out

shampoos, conditioners, creams,
wiping the bottles and muttering,
"Ziploc bags. You forgot the Ziploc bags."

Now she is combing her hair,
feeling for rollers, curlers, and pins.
He says, "We're coming into the depot."

"You mean station," she says. "Not depot."
"Depot," he says. She smiles.
"Where I come from you would never hear that."

"Depot," he says. "Depot."
"I heard that once in a movie," she says.
Feather clips chained to the gold clips

on her ears, sharp rings on both hands,
her hands waving, the nail polish drying,
and a woman who was once beautiful

lurches down the aisle fighting
a diaper bag and a baby,
everyone is eating chicken or chewing gum,

and beyond the window, the milkweed blows.
It's twilight. I was a seed once, he thinks.
I was a seed. It was that easy.

The Teachings of the Jade

The jade tree is all thumbs,
green ones. What she couldn't grow
if she had a mind to.

Admirer of elephants
and oaks, venerable
mathematician of the greenhouse,

constructing proofs so vast
she's forgotten the problem
and given herself to

abstruse branches of knowledge,
speaking in thick tongues,
urging emerald ears for mice

and knees that don't bend;
with mineral patience, she takes
her time, would make room

for me, if I were new enough
to know my place
under the family tree.

A Psalm for Vineyards

In the aging cellars, the wines are settling down.
Spirits destined to age in oak sleep
in cool barrels, their curved backs rising like loaves,
sauvignon blanc, sémillon, merlot
ripening, rack on rack. From the footbridge
spanning their stillness, I can see everything

and nothing. Twilight was born here.
What do spirits know of the world above?
The vineyards' calligraphy? The contredanses
of vine clasping vine? Hawks riding the wind
over stands of acacia? The cellist
on the terrace above who fastens *Bach's Greatest Hits*

with a clothespin and closes his eyes and plays?
They have survived the crushpit, the auger,
and fermentation to something less than themselves.
Born again, clarified, they go back to the world.
In the hives hidden under the plum trees, silence
is sealed in cells. I would feel at home there.

Onionlight

Sacks crammed with light, layer on luminous layer,
an underworld calendar, the peeled pages faintly lined
but printed without month or measure
and pure as the damp kiss of a pearl,

as if the rings in an old tree should suddenly separate
and bracelet the axe; I have stooped among onions all morning,
hunting these flightless birds as they perched among roots.
I have yanked them out by the tail

and dropped them into my bag like chickens
and pulled away the thin paper of their last days,
pale winegold, a silken globe, pungent,
striped with the pale longitude of silence.

Now over my door they shimmer in knobby garlands,
gregarious in chains like a string of lights
on the boardwalks of heaven where an old man
who loved his garden understands everything.

The Potato Picker

The plant lifts easily now, like an old tooth.
I can free it from the rows of low hills,
hills like the barrows of old kings

where months ago, before anything grew or was,
we hid the farsighted eyes of potatoes.
They fingered forth, blossomed, and shrank,

and did their dark business under our feet.
And now it's all over. Horse nettles dangle
their gold berries. Sunflowers, kindly giants

in their death-rattle turn stiff as streetlamps.
Pale cucumbers swell to alabaster lungs,
while marigolds caught in the quick frost

go brown, and the scarred ears of corn gnawed
by the deer lie scattered like primitive fish.
The lifeboats lifted by milkweed ride light

and empty, their sailors flying.
This is the spot. I put down my spade,
I dig in, I uncover the scraped knees

of children in the village of potatoes,
and the bald heads of their grandfathers.
I enter the potato mines.

The Weeder

Under the ground, all those voices:
the wet worm slipples past roots and opens tunnels,
grubs shiver in sunlight like sucked thumbs,
the locust splits his armor, goes forth a civilian,
and the roots tangle and clasp each other
like the hairs of a sleeper, hugging so hard
not even a big-toothed comb can part them.

By hand and by trowel I have picked my way
through the birth-rooms of weeds,
and the sleeping and waking of flowers,
and the roots of violets cracking their knuckles.
The lily of the valley lays down its life in miles
of pale cable, sending at intervals its green report.

When I get to the root of the matter,
the fat fingers of irises flash their soft blades
like the tail feathers of remarkable birds,
and the peonies turn on their taproots stained with sunset—
sherrydark corks that have ripened in deep cellars.
Galaxies of bulbs are rolling themselves into pearls.

I have dug, snipped, pulled, fed, taken, thrown away,
and what do the roots give me? Year after year they surrender
toy soldiers old children have lost in the grass.
Men of plastic, they do not become the grass.
This one hauls his machine gun under the roses;
gripped by its roots, he is taking aim at the dark.

God Enters the Swept Field

A field in ruins. Everything's coming due:
a scarf of starlings rinsing itself in the air,

pumpkins like quilted planets closing down,
coins tumbling out of the poplars' high rooms,

a party of maples basting an amber beast,
done to a turn on their black boughs. God's brooms

on hills honey-brushed and glowing like new loaves
scour and scrub the weeds, beaten thin and bright.

Let in the light.

Small Medicinal Poem

Only that which is truly oneself has the
power to heal.
—Carl Jung

With the ears of a deer I hear your story,
how you followed your father to the mountain,
how you followed him through juniper and birch,
how you found the clearing sacred to the deer people,
how their hooves printed hollow hearts in the mud,
how your father followed their prints,
how you dragged your feet,
how a hawk drew high circles around you,
how you looked away when your father said,
These are fresh tracks. Aim for the heart.

With the eyes of a hawk I see your story,
your father waiting for you to fire
at the doe who twitched into the clearing,
her fur slick with light, her ears pointing north.
You took aim at someone you wanted to wish on,
as welcome a guest as the first star.
Your father who loves you hissed, *Now! Now!*
And I think when you lowered your gun, half-weeping,
you found your own space. You became what you are.

With the tongue of a star, you tell me your story,
full of silence and distance and inner space.
What shall we call you in this chapter?
"He Who Cannot Eat Chicken Without Grieving."
"He Who Has Fallen in Love with the Moon."
"The Curate of Cats Who Has Understood Purring."
"He Whose Cat Spied a New Star and Told No One."
"He Who Carries a Glass Wand That Does Nothing."
"The Doctor of Divinities Who Have Fallen from Grace,"
or, in the language of the deer people: *he who saves.*

For Karen

She who came thousands of miles to say goodbye
sits in the plain room by her father's body.
It is her father and not her father
in the red-checked shirt her mother sent
like a birthday gift to the hushed house of the dead.
Terrible, saying goodbye to this flesh that can't hear,
to this mouth that can't answer.
Terrible, that a husband and wife linked
by thousands of days in the long light
of the studio where the only words spoken
flowed from each other as back and forth
they passed the paintings that deepened
under their hands and gathered themselves into books—
terrible that such parents should lose each other.
A week before her wedding, how terrible to be happy!
But she can't forget how her father loved to read
the night away and in the morning greet her,
"What do you think of this book? Isn't it
wonderful?" She pages through the good
times. He knows the ending.
Still, she tells him the whole story.

Little Elegy with Books and Beasts

in memory of Martin Provensen
(1916–1987)

I

Winters when the gosling froze to its nest
he'd warm it and carry it into the house praising
its finely engraved wings and ridiculous beak—
or sit all night by the roan mare, wrapping
her bruised leg, rinsing the cloths while his wife
read aloud from *Don Quixote,* and darkness hung
on the cold steam of her breath—
or spend three days laying a ladder for the hen
to walk dryshod into the barn.

Now the black cat broods on the porch.
Now the spotted hound meeting visitors, greets none.
Nestler, nurse, mender of wounded things,
he said he didn't believe in the body.
He lost the gander—elder of all their beasts
(not as wise as the cat but more beloved)—
the night of the first frost, the wild geese
calling—last seen waddling south
on the highway, beating his clipped wings.

II

He stepped outside through the usual door
and saw for the last time his bare maples
scrawling their cold script on the low hills
and the sycamore mottled as old stone
and the willows slurred into gold by the spring light,

and he noticed the boy clearing the dead brush—
old boughs that broke free under the cover of snow,
and he raised his hand, and a door in the air opened,
and what was left of him stumbled and fell
and lay at rest on the earth like a clay lamp
still warm whose flame was not nipped or blown
but lifted out by the one who lit it
and carried alive over the meadow—
that light by which we read, while he was here,
the chapter called Joy in the Book of Creation.

Poems from the Sports Page

"Buffalo Climbs out of Cellar"

"Will you have some sherry?" asked
the million-dollar baby-faced killer.

He filled my glass, and the whole room
sucked me into its sharkish smile.

"You're fond of hunting," I said.
"Did you shoot all those guys on the wall?"

He nodded and raised the cuff of his pants.
His left leg was ivory to the knee.

"That Bengal tiger was my first success.
Then I matched wits with a white whale

and won. After that I went in for elephants.
And then I heard about the last buffalo

in South Dakota. Very educated.
He speaks fluent Apache. He writes

by scratching his hooves in the dirt.
He's writing a history of the Civil War.

So naturally I took him alive. Day
and night I keep him locked in my cellar.

His breath heats this house all winter.
His heart charges all my rooms with light.

In my worst dreams I see them folding up
like a paper hat, and my dead tiger roaring

and my dead whale swimming off the wall
and my buffalo climbing out of the cellar."

"Saints Lose Back"

And there was complacency in heaven
for the space of half an hour,
and God said, Let every saint lose his back.

Let their wings and epaulettes shrivel,
and for immortal flesh give them flesh of man,
and for the wind of heaven a winter on earth.

The saints roared like the devil.
O my God, cried Peter, what have you done?
And God said,

Consider the back,
the curse of backache
the humpback's prayer.

Consider how thin a shell man wears.
The locust and crab are stronger than he.
Consider the back, how a rod breaks it.

Now consider the front, adorned with eyes,
cheeks, lips, breasts, all
the gorgeous weaponry of love.

Then consider the back, good for nothing
but to fetch and carry, crouch and bear
and finally to lie down on the earth.

O, my angels, my exalted ones,
consider the back,
consider how the other half lives.

"Field Collapses Behind Patullo"

THE FIRST SCROLL

To the chief eunuch of her Imperial Majesty
Marco Polo said,

"My country lies under yours.
If you dig a hole in your garden
you'll find me feeding the birds in mine.
Farewell!"

In the fourth moon, he weeded the lotus pond.
In the seventh moon, he cut the chrysanthemums.
In the ninth moon he covered their roots for the winter.
Farewell!

West of the Jade Girdle Bridge,
north of the Gate of White Peonies,
he dug a way out
from the ten thousand peacocks wanting their own way,

from the lotus, twisting its feet in the shallows
and the lizards like jokes cracked by an emerald.

Farewell.

THE SECOND SCROLL

When this eunuch died, another replaced him.
He, too, dug quietly toward the promised land.
The eunuch of the twenty-fifth generation
barely remembered the story.

What did he know of Marco Polo?
What did he know of New Jersey
and Patullo the chicken farmer, profoundly unlucky,
who on the sixth hour of the seventh moon

quarreled with his wife
and stomped toward the barn, with her calling
Go to hell
as the shovel broke through like a tooth

and the whole field collapsed behind him?

"Tigers Shake Up Pitchers Again"

First God made the waters of heaven.
Then he made two pitchers to hold it.
Then he said to his angel,

When I call for rain, dip rain from the sky
and pour it out on the fields of men.
From the gold pitcher comes plenty.
From the silver pitcher comes terror.

The angel was eager, slim, and alarmed.
How shall I, who am without weight
lift the pitchers that water the world?

Then God made two tigers.
He named the silver one thunder.
He named the gold one lightning
and loosed them both in the villages of the stars.

He made the flesh of the stars a poison.
He made the tigers strong and thirsty.
Listen to them, listen to them,
drunk with thirst, shaking the jugs of heaven.

Can you hear the wrath of silver?
Can you see the whips of gold?
Can you feel the rain on your face at last?

"Wayward Lass Wins Mother Goose"

"Good for nothing but sleeping late
  and sleeping around," said Humanmother,

"and for dropping her suitors like stitches
  and for singing off key with the cats

  and for sitting on eggs and letting
  the hens take their ease, and for

  skipping with lambs instead of
  shearing them and running

  with water instead of fetching it
  home from the well."

"Let her sleep in the sty," said Humanfather.
"Let her gossip with ganders."

  And they turned her out into the yard
  and she lay in the straw, listening,

  and Goosemother sang,
"O, my wild flower, my featherless daughter,

  I bless your tongue and its wayward verses,
  I bless your mouth and its burden of nonsense.

  I give you my faith in the kindness of butchers
  and my foolishness, which has made me immortal.

  I give you the keys to my queer kingdom."

"Stars Nip Wings"

"Sun and moon go down, my dear.
  What matters when they rise?
  The falcon bears us all away,
  the beautiful, the wise,
  and none returns to tell the rest
  where that creature flies."

"*Sun and moon will hatch, my dear,*
  and the stars nip our wings,
  if ever I forget my love,
  the lowly sparrow sings.
  Can you and I do less, my dear,
  than simple, lawless things?"

"Divine Child Rolls On"

Lullaby, my sparrow.
Cipher, make your mark
in the Book of Being.
Fly into the dark,

passenger of the planet.
Sun and stars are gone.
The Divine Child find you,
bless you, and roll on.

from

A Nancy Willard Reader

(1991)

One for the Road

On the old bicycle the plumber brought me
Saint Christopher gleams by the traffic bell.
"Good as new." He tapped a rusty fender.
"The girl who rode it moved to Florida.
She was some kind of teacher, too," he grinned.

No baskets, saddlebags, license, or lights.
Eight novels crammed into my backpack—
excessive as a life vest stuffed with stones—
I pedal two miles to the travel agent
to pay for my son's airline ticket home.

Twenty years ago I jogged to market
bearing the light burden of him, bobbing
against my back. Singing to rooks and jays,
he dipped his head under the sky's wing.
He was lighter than my dictionary.

On the threshold, when I set him down,
my muscles quivered, light flooded my bones.
I was a still lake holding up the sky.
Now in his empty room, I hang the map
that flopped out of the *National Geographic*.

Start with what you know, I tell my students.
Detroit, New York, Ann Arbor, Battle Creek—
the roads that spider off from towns I know

are red as arteries that serve the heart
and bring fresh news to all its distant cities,

Madison, Minneapolis–St. Paul.
At his first solo flight away from home
wearing the new jeans he'd bought for school,
his father gave him a gold medal. "Given
for good conduct all the years we had you,

and for good luck." A talisman, a blessing,
friendly as butter: Christopher, untarnished,
bearing the magic child across the stream.

from

Among Angels

1995

The Winged Ones

No birthday gift whiter or stranger
than this large pair of wings
my son bought on Amsterdam Avenue.
Pressed from celluloid, thick
as a toenail; two basins
that crease the morning light
in deeply stamped feathers.
A fossil from heaven. The tag
warns: "Not intended for flight."

"One size fits all," you assure me
and unfold the intricate harness
and buckle the wings to my body
that never sprang from a sill
or plotted the air through a thicket
or turned on the lathe of a wind
that could snuff out the breath in me
and toss me out of my garden.
There's no finer sight in summer

than yourself wearing them,
making the rounds in Eden,
inspecting the spotted throat
of the lily, the fern's plumage,
stepping behind your girl
quiet as mint on the move
in the woods where the owl lives
and hugging her where the gate was,
angel who forgives.

Photographing the Angels

for Lilo Raymond

The first angel you brought us stands high
over a city which does not appear in the picture,
yet no one who sees the angel doubts
the city is there. He folds his arms,
swathed in stone, and turns his blank gaze to heaven.
His hair seems newly hatched, snaky curls,
his wings chunky as bread, the feathers cast
from a mold like a big cookie.
When he clarified himself in your darkroom,
you saw what the lens did not show you:
a fly perched on an angel's head.

The second angel you brought us slumps
on a wall by a dump which does not appear in the picture.
Broken from the start, she will never be whole
except in the eye of the beholder
who praises the mosaic painter's art,
though bricks and cement cake
the hem of her robe like a scab. Her head on her hand,
her eyes closed, her wings ashen, she drags her dark torch
on the ground like a broken umbrella.
She has sunk so far into herself not even you
could bring her to brightness,

though you brought her out of hiding.
Those years you photographed white curtains blowing
in white rooms over beds rumpled like ice floes,

you were honing your eye for what might dwell
in space as pure and simple as an egg.
The third angel you gave us holds a rose
so lightly it must have grown in a bed
where each rose chooses the hand that plucks it
and turns its open gaze on what rises and sets,
like a camera gathering the souls of pears,
the piety of eggs, the light in a dark room. Angels.

Angels Among the Servants

*Build a chair as if an angel
were going to sit on it.*
—Thomas Merton

St. Zita, patron saint
of scrub buckets and brooms,
spiritual adviser to mops,
protector of charwomen,
chambermaids, cooks,
those who wait on us
and mend our ways,

for forty-eight years you
lit the morning fire
in the dark kitchen
of Fatinelli of Lucca
and baked his bread,
till the Sunday you knew
you could not serve

two masters and did not open
the bins of flour or unlock
the treasures of yeast
and water. Telling no one,
you trudged off to Mass,
still wearing his keys
on your belt.

And while you opened your mouth
for the wafer, a coin
minted from moonlight,

angels arrived in aprons
and mixed light and salt,
and kneaded loaf after loaf,
punching them down

for their own good,
and praised the mystery
of bread, which rises to meet
its maker. But who
is the servant here?
The loaf will not rise
till the baker follows
the rules set down by the first loaf

for the ancient order of bread.
St. Zita, bless the fire
that boils water, the air
that dries clothes, and keys
that have lost their doors:
may angels keep them
from the deep river.

Jacob Boehme and the Angel

A light in his workshop
unlocked his sleep, and fearing
a fire the shoemaker
ran barefoot

across the snow
and opened the door.
The angel was waiting
on sapphire feet.

The shoemaker measured,
marked, and cut. Soles,
foxing, and tips fell
from the burnished calfskin,

laid to rest on the wooden last,
like a foot unfit for walking.
He crimped and stitched,
and the angel watched,

and the shop grew hot
as a foundry. He threaded
his needle with fire,
and with fire nailed heel

to sole, and with fire
pulled the shoes
from the last. The angel
put them on,

first the left,
then the right,
stepping so softly
even the snow did not speak of it.

Visitation in a Pewter Dish

When Jacob finished stitching
the seventh pair of shoes,
his hands smelled of new
leather, as if the calf
whose mortal part he'd shaped
wanted to claim him.

Five blind bells woke
the fields at the edge of town.
Men left off binding the rain
into shocks of gold and rested
at noon under the plane trees.
　　　Angelus Domini—
The cows were happy boulders,

and Jacob saw, in a pewter dish
on a dirty table, seven angels
lapped in their own light.
Prove all things, sang the dish.
Hold fast to that which is good.
Jacob said nothing, only watched

with great joy. Wheels clattered
on the cobbled streets.
Two customers paid with gold,
two with wool, three with pork,
and the shoes took their first steps
out of the fields of light.

Acknowledgments and Permissions

Some of the poems in this collection were originally
published in the following:

ATLANTA REVIEW: "Winston Farm"

NEW ENGLAND REVIEW: "The Patience of Bathtubs"

THE NEW YORKER: "Guesthouse, Union City, Michigan" (May 11, 1992),
"The Exodus of Peaches" (July 27, 1992),
"At the Optometrist's" (September 7, 1992),
"The Alligator Wrestler" (April 26, 1993),
and "The Winged Ones" (October 31, 1994)

YANKEE MAGAZINE: "Flea Market"

Poems from Skin of Grace, copyright © 1967 and 1995 by
Nancy Willard, published by University of Missouri Press

Poems from A Nancy Willard Reader
published by University Press of New England.

The following poems by Nancy Willard are reprinted by
permission of the publications in which they previously appeared:

THE AMICUS JOURNAL: "Sand Shark" (fall 1992)

THE BELOIT POETRY JOURNAL: "The Garden of Stone Cabbages,"
"Uninvited Houses," and "The Wisdom of the Jellyfish"

CALIBAN: "A Conversation Phrase Book for Angels"

FIELD: "In Praise of the Puffball," "A Member of the Wedding,"
"Memory Hat," "Swimming to China,"
"A Very Still Life," and "The Wisdom of the Geese"

LAPIS: "Cold Water" (September 1995)

THE LAUREL REVIEW: "Still Life with Drive-in"

NEW LETTERS: "The Burning at Neilson's Farm" (59:3, spring 1993)

PASSAGES NORTH: "The Bell Ringers of Kalamazoo" (vol. 14, no. 2)

Ten poems from 19 Masks for the Naked Poet,
twenty poems from Household Tales of Moon and Water,
and five poems from Among Angels
published by Harcourt Brace & Company

Seven poems from The Ballad of Biddy Early, copyright
© 1989 by Nancy Willard, and twenty-seven poems
from Water Walker, copyright © 1989 by Nancy Willard,
published by Alfred A. Knopf, Inc.

Seventeen poems from Carpenter of the Sun
published by W. W. Norton & Company.

Excerpt from In the American Grain by William Carlos Williams,
copyright © 1933 by William Carlos Williams.
Reprinted by permission of New Directions Publishing Corp.

A Note About the Author

*Nancy Willard grew up in Ann Arbor, Michigan, and
was educated at the University of Michigan and Stanford
University. She has written two novels, four books of
stories and essays, and ten books of poetry.
A winner of the Devins Memorial Award, she
has had NEA grants in both fiction and poetry.
A previous book,* Water Walker, *was nominated for
the National Book Critics Circle Award.
For* A Visit to William Blake's Inn, *she won
the Newbery Medal.
She teaches in the English department
at Vassar College.*

A Note on the Type

The text of this book was set in Bembo, a facsimile
of a typeface cut by Francesco Griffo for Aldus Manutius,
the celebrated Venetian printer, in 1495.
The face was named for Pietro Cardinal Bembo, the author
of the small treatise entitled De Ætna in which
it first appeared. The present-day version of Bembo was
introduced by the Monotype Corporation of London in 1929.
Sturdy, well balanced, and finely proportioned,
Bembo is a face of rare beauty and great legibility
in all of its sizes.

Composed by North Market Street Graphics,
Lancaster, Pennsylvania

Printed and bound by Quebecor Printing,
Fairfield, Pennsylvania

Designed by Misha Beletsky